D0626618

How To Be Confident

Prentice Hall LIFE

If life is what you make it, then making it better starts here.

What we learn today can change our lives tomorrow. It can change our goals or change our minds; open up new opportunities or simply inspire us to make a difference. That's why we have created a new breed of books that do more to help you make more of *your* life.

Whether you want more confidence or less stress, a new skill or a different perspective, we've designed *Prentice Hall Life* books to help you to make a change for the better. Together with our authors we share a commitment to bring you the brightest ideas and best ways to manage your life, work and wealth.

In these pages we hope you'll find the ideas you need for the life *you* want. Go on, help yourself.

It's what you make it

* * *

How To Be Confident

Using the power of NLP

David Molden and Pat Hutchinson

PEARSON

Prentice Hall

LIFE

Harlow, England • London • New York • Boston • San Francisco • Toronto • Sydney • Singapore • Hong Kong
Tokyo • Seoul • Taipei • New Delhi • Cape Town • Madrid • Mexico City • Amsterdam • Munich • Paris • Milan

PEARSON EDUCATION LIMITED

Edinburgh Gate
Harlow CM20 2JE
Tel: +44 (0)1279 623623
Fax: +44 (0)1279 431059
Website: www.pearsoned.co.uk

First published in Great Britain in 2008

© Pearson Education Limited 2008

The rights of David Molden and Pat Hutchinson to be identified as authors of this work have been asserted by them in accordance with the Copyright, Designs and Patents Act 1988.

All rights reserved. No part of this publication may be reproduced, stored in a retrieval system, or transmitted in any form or by any means, electronic, mechanical, photocopying, recording or otherwise, without either the prior written permission of the publisher or a licence permitting restricted copying in the United Kingdom issued by the Copyright Licensing Agency Ltd, Saffron House, 6–10 Kirby Street, London EC1N 8TS. This book may not be lent, resold, hired out or otherwise disposed of by way of trade in any form of binding or cover other than that in which it is published, without the prior consent of the Publishers.

ISBN: 978-0-273-71809-3

British Library Cataloguing-in-Publication Data
A catalogue record for this book is available from the British Library

Library of Congress Cataloging-in-Publication Data
Molden, David.
   How to be confident : using the power of NLP / David Molden and Pat Hutchinson
      p. cm.
   ISBN 978 0 273 71809 3 (pbk)
 1. Self-confidence. 2. Neurolinguistic programming. I. Hutchinson, Pat. II. Title.
   BF575.S39M65 2008
   158.1--dc22
                            2008034260

10 9 8 7 6 5 4 3 2 1
12 11 10 09 08

Designed by Design Deluxe, Bath
Illustrations by David Berger

Typeset in 10pt IowanOldStyle by 3
Printed and bound in Great Britain by Clays Ltd, Bungay, Suffolk

The publisher's policy is to use paper manufactured from sustainable forests.

Contents

About the authors   vii

Introduction   1

01 Reach out for real confidence   7

02 Self-awareness is the key to confidence   23

03 Believe in yourself   53

04 Stay on the field, 'Keep the shutters open'   69

05 Connect with others   93

06 Create empowering feelings   107

07 Step outside your comfort zone   125

08 Who is knocking your confidence?   143

09 Confident body, confident mind   161

10 Imagine successful outcomes   179

11 The confidence challenge   191

About the authors

David Molden is a personal development trainer and coach and Chartered Fellow of the CIPD. Since 1995 he has introduced NLP techniques to thousands of people from all walks of life including entrepreneurs, managers, sports professionals and children, in their pursuit of personal success.

David has a zest for life and an unremitting sense of fun. He maintains a high level of fitness and mind-body balance by training in Tai Chi Chuan and has an interest in ancient wisdom and its relevance for today's society.

David is a Director with Quadrant 1 International, an NLP training and development company. He has appeared on TV and radio, and is the author of several other Pearson books, including *Managing with the Power of NLP*, *NLP Business Masterclass*, *Beat Your Goals* and co-author with Pat Hutchinson on the *Brilliant NLP* book and audio CD.

Pat Hutchinson has a rich background of experience as an entrepreneur and leader of sales and marketing teams. She is an NLP trainer and coach and a Director with Quadrant 1 International.

Pat's combination of leading edge personal change skills with a sense of practicality makes learning and applying NLP easy and enjoyable. Her ability to focus and get 'straight to the heart of the matter' makes her a highly sought after trainer and coach. She has an enviable record of results with both individuals and business groups. Pat is co-author with David Molden on the *Brilliant NLP* book and audio CD.

Both David and Pat can be contacted via info@quadrant1.com

Introduction

LUCAN
LIBRARY
TEL. 6

"What lies behind us and what lies before us are tiny matters compared to what lies within us."
Ralph Waldo Emerson, nineteenth-century American scholar and self-help pioneer

Goodbye low self-esteem, hello confidence

We have been running our tried-and-tested personal development courses based on NLP for 15 years now and, of the individuals and organisations we help, a staggering 80 per cent had issues relating to self-confidence. Our experience has shown us that what people appear to lack – and want more than anything – is to overcome low self-esteem and achieve goals that mean so much to them. Can you relate to a loss or lack of confidence that leads you down a spiral staircase of embarrassment, fear and even shaking and palpitations?

If this is you, then prepare to break out of that spiral!

This book will show you how to use specially-targetted NLP techniques to become CONFIDENT – any-where, any time.

"Make the most of yourself, for that is all there is of you."

'OK,' you ask, 'how?' Well, you already have it within you, whether you believe it or not, to achieve so many things. As the American free thinker Ralph Waldo Emerson (whom we have already quoted above) said insightfully, 'Make the most of yourself, for that is all there is of you.' All you need is a way of releasing your true potential and NLP has a proven track record of helping people around the world do just this.

NLP: what it is and how it works

NLP stands for Neurolinguistic Programming which does sound quite jargony; but look at it like this:

neuro is to do with the workings of the brain and our thoughts, emotions and memory

linguistic is about the way we communicate our thoughts both verbally and non-verbally such as through 'body language'

programming refers to the habitual programmes of thinking and behaviour we run and re-run every day – in other words our habits. Some programmes (or habits) will certainly deliver positive outcomes for you, whilst others may not, and this is where NLP does its work: it reprogrammes your habits so that you can have more positive experiences, more often, in all aspects of your life.

NLP was developed by Richard Bandler and John Grinder in the 1970s. They developed a range of techniques and models that essentially **dis-abled** negative thoughts and behaviour, which we all are prone to, and **en-abled** new and constructive thoughts, memories, emotions and language to build self-improvement and self-worth. NLP was adopted and adapted by business professionals, entrepreneurs, coaches and therapists from the 1980s.

"NLP reprogrammes your habits so that you can have more positive experiences, more often, in all aspects of your life."

Why NLP for confidence?

If we all had sunny dispositions and oozed confidence naturally we would not need NLP. But life is not like that and, even if we are confident in one aspect of our lives, that does not mean we might not lack confidence in another.

So what stops you, or anyone else from gaining confidence? The answer is *your feelings*. Now that includes very much the 'hang ups' we all get – fear, anxiety, self-doubt, depression which are all there to trip you up and stop you feeling confident.

What NLP does is get to the cause of those 'limiting' feelings that act as a block on your capability, and help you open up to all kinds of possibilities and make whatever changes are necessary so you can *feel the way you want to feel*. NLP compels you to pursue what you really want with vigour and verve.

"NLP is very effective at getting to the cause of your feelings and making whatever changes are necessary so you can feel the way you want to feel."

Take AIM now

Whatever you want to be confident at – managing a meeting, social chit-chat, supercharging a career, or driving a car – NLP has tools to help you achieve your aim. We encourage this through our own AIM – a set of targets based on our longstanding professional experience and practical NLP course techniques and exercises which we spell out as follows:

1 Become **A**ware of how you habitually create feelings around confidence.

2 Begin to think more confidently using positive **I**ntention to power your new-found self-belief.

3 Use a range of techniques to create a compelling sense of **M**otivation in yourself – act confidently and achieve what you really want.

It is as simple as ABC because it is based on the premise that:

1 You need to create self-**A**wareness (pay more attention to the world and what people say, how they say it, body language, tone of voice, etc.

AWARENESS

SELF BELIEF

CONFIDENCE

2 You need self-**B**elief (finding your limitations to goal setting).

3 From A and B will come C – self-**C**onfidence (empowering yourself).

At the end of each chapter we have included a key NLP principle – a 'trigger' or hook-line – upon which NLP is built. Conclude each confidence-building chapter by reading and repeating each trigger aloud, and check they resonate with what you have learnt before proceeding to the next stage.

And here is the first.

NLP TRIGGER

YOU HAVE ALL THE RESOURCES
YOU NEED TO SUCCEED

- Read and re-read this trigger point: if it helps say it aloud in a confident tone.

- You were born with the same potential to be confident as anyone else.

- As you grew and acquired experiences you adopted beliefs and values about what is possible and what is not.

- The way you have interpreted your experiences has acted to either empower you, or limit you – but it is all just interpretation.

- Because of this you need to learn only how to reverse the limitation process and your innate confident resources will emerge.

01

Reach out for real confidence

"Argue for your limitations and, sure enough, they're yours."

Richard Bach author of *Illusions*

What you are going to discover

- There is false and misplaced confidence, and then there is real confidence.

- People you think are confident may be simply 'good at their job'.

- Real confidence can be transferred from one scenario to another quite different scenario with equal self-awareness and self-belief.

In our work we meet literally hundreds of people who are confident in certain scenarios but have their confidence knocked when they step into unfamiliar territory.

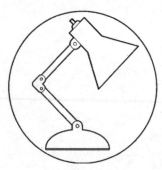

"Real confidence is being comfortable enough with yourself to enter unfamiliar territory and have a go."

Take this example:

Case study: Brimming with false confidence

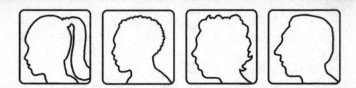

Michael insisted he had loads of confidence. His friends told him so and he was always the life and soul of the party. He could talk to anyone and did not mind people having a laugh at his expense. Michael was good at his insurance job and quickly rose to the level of manager. Pleased with his progress he set about organising his team with great enthusiasm, determined to show his own line manager that he could be trusted with his new role. But within a few weeks of taking on his new role Michael sought our NLP course claiming to have no confidence as a leader.

Michael, like the many others we meet on our NLP courses, had been confusing confidence with familiarity. It is easy to be confident when you know people well, or when you have been doing a job or hobby for some time. Your expectations are met and there are few surprises to throw you off course.

The more you do something, the easier it seems to get.

What you are often describing by the word 'confident' is someone who is familiar with a particular task or situation, has experienced it before, and has become adept at dealing with it. But that is not 'real' confidence.

Real confidence

Real confidence is being comfortable enough with yourself to enter unfamiliar territory and have a go, being able to extend your confidence from one scenario to another. When you lack confidence it is as though you are hiding from whatever you are facing, whilst at the same time seeking a way of feeling better about yourself. In an attempt to keep the feelings at bay you will manipulate the situation, and so the pattern continues. So real confidence also means replacing a lack of confidence with a powerful 'bring it on' attitude.

The irrational fear of failure

So what stops you from finding the confidence you seek? There may be any number of situations where you lack confidence, but they all have one thing in common – they will all be rooted to some kind of fear relating to your ability to succeed. The roots may be long, entangled and reaching deep into your unconscious mind, and this is why feelings of low confidence often seem irrational. It is easy to tell yourself that you should be able to do something well, but when the feelings of fear or anxiety kick in, no amount of rationalising is going to save you.

The comparison game can magnify a lack of confidence

Comparison is a very useful way of noticing differences between how you approach a task and how another person approaches the same task. If you copy and learn from what people do and apply your learning, you can benefit from their approach. However, if you pigeon-hole a person you are observing as 'confident' you may feel inadequate by comparison (as many people who lack confidence do). Similarly, if you label a person you are observing as having, say, 'low self-esteem' or some such negative, you may feel more adequate by comparison.

But what are your observations based on? All you are doing is creating an illusion that you are better or worse than some other person you have happened to observe. Think of the times you have observed someone from afar and made an instant judgement about them, possibly from their appearance, only to have your judgement changed when you eventually got to speak with them.

Measuring yourself against other people is a common way to magnify a lack of confidence. The mind has the capacity to compare high, or compare low, depending on whether you are prone to positive or negative thinking. What you see, and how you compare yourself with what you see, is only in your imagination. It is not real. It is an illusion.

Confident scenarios

It is also amazing how people who demonstrate outward confidence in one scenario are often hiding all sorts of perceived deficiencies and insecurities in another scenario. This can be traced to what in NLP is called the Focus of Interest. There are five key ones:

1 People.

2 Places.

3 Activities.

4 Things.

5 Information.

So if you lack confidence in, say, 5 Information you might say, 'Oh, I could never learn that, I'd never remember all that,' or if it were 2 Places, you might think, 'Oh, I could never go there, I only go here,' or with 1 People, 'Who's coming? I need to know who'll be there before I decide to go to the party because if so-and-so's going I won't feel good about . . .' The converse is true too: if information is your strength then you use it as a prop, 'I'm very good at information so that is where I spend most of my time.'

A classic example of 4 Things or gadget focus is the awkward New Year's Eve dinner party where on the strike of midnight all the guests send and receive their mobile text messages but cannot wish Happy New Year to the guest opposite them. They relate to things more than people (they might be happier relating in the virtual world of 'second life') and their lack of confidence is in their social life.

Masking a lack of confidence
Shyness and nerves

People go to great lengths to mask their lack of confidence. Sometimes it is done deliberately and sometimes it is a deeper unconscious process.

Case study: Off-piste skills

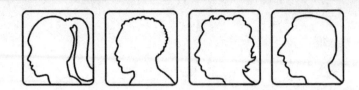

Darren loves to ski. He is so skilled at skiing he does not think twice about going off-piste through trees or attacking heavy mogul black runs while revelling in the treacherous route down the craggy slopes. If James Bond comes to mind you have the right image. You might think, therefore, that he is a confident person, but you would be wrong. He is just a good skier. He is very shy and nervous at the thought of socialising with people he does not know, and feels downright awkward and anxious in the company of strangers.

Darren's problem stemmed from a belief he held around 'small talk'. He didn't believe he could do it and had convinced himself that it was not important. This belief helped him justify his 'avoidance' behaviour (making the judgement, 'you're not worth talking to so I won't talk to you') as he watched his wife and her friends engaging in small talk. He felt it just was not for him. However, Darren wanted to expand his business and knew that he had to take on a much more proactive role engaging potential customers. Building rapport with such people was crucial to his success. We encouraged Darren to reframe his view of 'small talk' to that of 'big talk' and gave him some skills and techniques for building rapport. As a result he is now able to engage anyone in conversation with ease (see Chapter 5).

Case study: Sharp dressed man

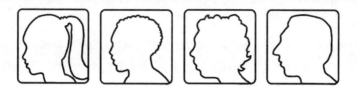

Barry is a company director in his mid-forties. He has managed to climb to the top of the corporate ladder displaying all the trappings of success. He is a bright, fast-thinking individual who wears expensive designer suits to work. One day he mentioned that he had been in the high street in his local town at the weekend. It was a hot sunny day and he had dashed out from working around the house to buy some DIY materials. He was dressed in his shorts and casual gear only to be horrified as he noticed a member of his staff walking his way. Not wishing to be seen in his 'scruffs' he hid in a shop doorway until this person had passed.

Barry's example demonstrates another way we mask lack of confidence by what is called 'distracter' behaviour.[1] In other words, 'If I start to feel vulnerable I will cause a distraction and change the topic.' A smart suit can give the appearance of being formal, important or serious, thus distracting others from noticing a feeling of insecurity.

His behaviour was born from 'fear'. Why would he not want his staff to see him in his 'scruffs'? Would they laugh? Does he think they put him on some kind of pedestal? Does he think they believe he does not have an existence outside of the office? Does his power within the company work only when he is wearing his suit? It does not matter which question you ask, such behaviour displays a 'fear' of some kind. Barry was

---

[1] The term was coined by Virginia Satir, a famous family therapist in *New Peoplemaking* (1989), Science and Behavior Books, whose work has implications for groups and teams as well as families.

unaware how much he had been using his stylish clothes to mask his lack of confidence amongst a team of highly professional people.

Case study: Sweet talkin' guy

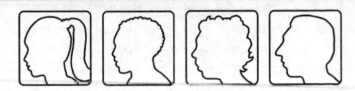

Peter indulged in distracter behaviour of a different kind. When he was with colleagues and friends he felt the need to continually tell jokes and play the fool. His friends thought of him as a great chap and he was always the first one to be invited to a social event. What they did not know was that Peter had a very poor opinion of himself. He was overweight and was struggling to shed the pounds. It seemed that the more he tried the lower his opinion of himself dropped and the more jokes he felt he had to tell to keep his friends.

Peter's first step to finding confidence was to create an awareness that his distracter behaviour of incessant joke telling had become a habit – realising this was the first step in the A-I-M journey, **A** for awareness. From self-obsession about thinking how awful he felt (low self-esteem) and disconnecting himself from the outside world he was now intent (**I**, intention) on keeping his focus on what was happening in the outside world. He was moved to act (**M**, move to action) in more effective ways through this different perspective.

The self-obsession cycle

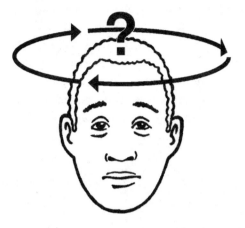

So how often do you make yourself the object of your thoughts? The more you worry about whether you will be perceived as this or that kind of person, the more you tell yourself how inadequate you are, the more you put yourself down, the more self-obsessed you become.

"People who are confident in most scenarios do not need to ask themselves if they are confident."

People who are confident in most scenarios do not need to ask themselves if they are confident. It is the same as asking yourself if you are happy. If you have to ask yourself, then you are probably not.

So you can begin to shake off your feelings of low confidence by keeping your focus on other things – turn your attention outward and pay attention to other people. Be more curious to know and learn – forget how you are feeling and concentrate on what you are going to do.

The concept of curiosity

Here is an easy-to-follow try-out exercise to give you more control over your attention (which is the route out of self-obsession).

You will find more exercises in later chapters but try this one now to get a feel about how your mental focus and concentration can really work to give you **awareness** as the first step to **intention** and **motivation**. This is where you will feel the true power of NLP. Since most of us seem unable to control our attention fully and suffer from distraction and general mind clutter, this is a useful technique to have up your sleeve.

Exercise: To break out of the self-obsession cycle and develop curiosity

1 Sit quietly close to a window.

2 Choose an object that you can see clearly from the window, in this exercise let us say a tree (but it could be a building, and so on).

3 Begin to focus on the detail. Notice the trunk.

4 Now notice the bark, the shape of the branches and the leaves coming off those branches.

5 Study the shapes and patterns formed by the leaves.

6 Are there birds in the tree? If so be curious about them. What are they doing? Are they singing? What colour are they? How big are they? How many can you see?

7 Concern yourself only with facts. Resist the temptation to conjecture. Focus only on what you see **not** what you think you

might be seeing. For example, 'I see a brown bird in the tree' is fact. 'The bird looks frightened', is conjecture about the way the bird might be feeling.

8 Focus on the tree and its ecosystem from its outline shape to its inner core and do this for several minutes.

9 Notice how you feel when you have finished focusing on something totally outside of yourself.

Strategies to mask low confidence

If, like many people, you have lacked confidence from time to time, you will probably have dealt with it in one of two ways. After first imagining how difficult or impossible the task before you is, and projecting a negative outcome, you are likely to have adopted:

1 **A superficial strategy** to try and feel confident, such as:

- dressing smartly

- memorising information you can use to impress people, or

- talking constantly to prevent uncomfortable silences.

People with low self-esteem usually have a well-practised act which forms a regular habit and can be called upon to protect them from any uncertain situation.

People who use superficial strategies to mask their low confidence often put on a good show, but underneath there are strong feelings of unease.

So the consequence of using a superficial strategy to mask your feelings is that whilst you may feel you look confident,

REACH OUT FOR REAL CONFIDENCE

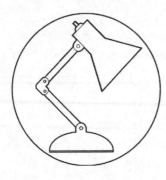

underneath you are shaking like a leaf, and the mask is only temporary.

"You will look for ways to make yourself feel good, and create a very temporary state of pleasure ... These good feelings have nothing to do with confidence, and everything to do with feeling satisfied and comfortable."

2 **A distracter strategy** also known as 'taking a comfort break' such as:

- eating chocolate
- tidying up, or
- doing something routine and mundane, smoking, drinking or drug taking.

When you feel low generally, you will look for ways to make yourself feel good, and create a very temporary state of pleasure. You can always succeed at tidying your desk, ironing or doing the washing up. These good feelings have nothing to do with confidence, and everything to do with feeling satisfied and comfortable. They never result in increased confidence; on the contrary, they create a barrier to actually dealing with the situation that causes you to feel low and the 'root' problem is never 'weeded out' (so the same old feelings continue).

So the consequence of taking a comfort break is that you are avoiding certain situations and making yourself feel even worse into the bargain.

Make your imagination – and illusions – work for you

Like all people, you are very good at creating images in your mind – the question is, are they working for you or against you? Perhaps you could use the power of an image or illusion to build confidence? We have touched on how you can create a negative image or illusion by comparing yourself with someone else, and then feel bad; so why can't you create images that make you feel good?

Think back to a time when you were listening to someone tell you about a memorable experience they had. As you were listening did you imagine what you would have done in that situation? Did your personal version end up the same way as the person telling you what happened for them, or something different?

We are all very good at listening to a story and making up a personalised scenario in our mind where we can conjecture specific outcomes based on our own past experiences. This is how we make sense of the world, by comparing what we are experiencing to something we have experienced in the past and filling in the gaps with conjecture and assumption (which is nothing but illusion).

So what is reality? Is your reality, my reality? We experience the world and our relationships through our perception of reality; we trust our senses; we trust our illusions so let us make them positive.

We cannot change whatever happened in the past but we can change our imagining or illusion of it.

Negative feelings, such as frustration, anxiety and anger, block rational thinking. The way you feel then becomes a higher priority than how well you perform in the situation before you. On the other hand, when the feelings are positive they will help you

access your rational mind and motivate you to 'get on with it' (whatever it is), and help you make appropriate behavioural choices.

"The way you feel about yourself will depend on the degree of positive or negative emotions you have attached to your experience. Lack of confidence is an illusion that you keep alive through an emotional connection with your memory of an event."

Exercise: To create positive illusion

So it is time to throw out the negative illusions that make you feel bad and create an illusion that will give you warm, positive feelings and make you feel good about yourself. Positive or negative, the process is the same, but it is time to be aware of positive thoughts.

Warm up: be curious and non-judgemental

Start by being curious about other people's behaviour. Resist the temptation to put a meaning on it and therefore a judgement. Notice what they do and how they get their results. If you judge others you are likely to also judge yourself. Instead develop curiosity to notice things without making a judgement. The instant you make a judgement you close down the possibility that it could mean something else. The act of judging others is often an expression of self-obsession. The sooner you stop judging the more you will notice and the better you will begin to feel.

Step 1. Focus your attention on a future situation affecting you. Think about a situation now that causes you to feel low in confidence. This could be an interview, an exam, a meeting, a dental appointment. Take a few moments to project it into your mind.

Step 2. Now stand or sit up straight. As you look up to your right, begin to imagine how you will look as a confident person. Notice how you are standing, and how others are responding positively towards you.

Step 3. Turn this picture into a movie and run it through to a successful outcome, smiling as you do so. Make your illusion really lifelike. Turn up the colour, brightness and contrast of your internal movie.

Step 4. Begin to move your attention away from you and towards the other people in this situation. Tell yourself that it is not about you (that would be self-obsessive) but rather it is about the contribution you are making.

Step 5. Bring your image closer and sense the positive feelings growing as you do so. Allow this positive feeling to build and move to every part of your body.

Step 6. Now say to yourself, in a confident-sounding voice tone, how much you are looking forward to getting started with this situation.

And relax. What you have done here is create a positive illusion that creates a positive and motivational feeling. Practise this exercise a number of times over the next few days so you get used to having this feeling more often. It will eventually become an automatic process producing confident behaviour.

NLP TRIGGER

THE MAP IS NOT THE TERRITORY

■ If you want to drive from A to B you can use a map or punch in the postcode on a SatNav to show you which route to use. But the map is not the territory and does not show the traffic, the roadworks, diversions, visibility and all kinds of other experiences you will have en route. In a similar way, the meanings you put on your experiences are only your interpretations – yet you might act as if this were the real territory and believe it to be the map.

■ Everyone has a unique map of the territory we tend to call reality.

■ Your personal map, your reality, results from filtering every single experience through the following:

> your past experience
>
> your memories
>
> your beliefs
>
> your values
>
> your language.

■ Is your map due for an update?

02

Self-awareness is the key to confidence

"Nature is not kind to creatures without self-awareness."
Moshe Feldenkrais, founder of the Feldenkrais method of self-awareness through movement

What you have discovered so far

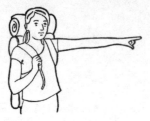

■ The feeling of confidence is a 'mask' and one that changes depending on the angle from which you are viewing it.

■ You may consider someone as confident but this is only a perception you have built up.

■ Your feelings become habitual so that your 'take' on confidence is simply conditioned by a habit based on past experience and your interpretation of it.

What you are going to discover

■ Self-awareness is the first step to building confidence.

■ You can then use this awareness to create real significant change that is going to leave you feeling so much more confident in all the things you do.

■ From here we are going to make your illusion give you warm positive feelings.

Can you measure confidence?

People talk about 'bags of confidence'. How much goes into a bag? The size of the bag is also a perception depending on the viewpoint of the onlooker. The word 'confidence' is a verb that has been converted into a noun, that is, 'to be confident' becomes 'to have confidence'. It is not tangible and it cannot be measured other than by individual perception.

Case study: Oi, ref!

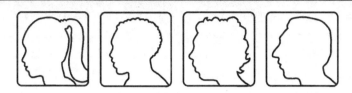

Some time ago a relative was refereeing a football match between Millwall and Luton Town. The stand behind one goal became overcrowded and the supporters began to spill onto the pitch. The situation soon got out of hand and missiles were thrown at the players so the referee took the decision to take the players off. In the ensuing minutes the club managers decided that the best way to regain the peace was to ask the referee to make an appeal over the loud speaker system. The referee took the microphone and confidently told the crowd that he wanted to continue with the match and was sure they wanted it to continue too. He went on to say that the only way he would allow the players back onto the pitch was if the supporters returned to their seats.

It worked. The crowd went back, the players returned and the match was completed. The national sports headlines the following day heralded the referee as the 'Black Knight'. So how much confidence did it take to pick up the microphone and do what he did? Was it bags or was he just doing his job? Of course it is all a question of perception – it is an illusion based on the viewpoint of the onlooker.

What makes you tick?

What gets you up and going in the morning? And what do the values you place on your personal, social and work life, and by which you naturally function, say about you? We call your personal approaches to all the various situations you encounter, metaprogammes, and in a non-jargony sense they can provide a very useful personal profile and insight into how you behave and react – how you tick. It is about your personality or aspects of your personality. For example, you might be someone who intrinsically gets the big picture, the overall idea and concept, or you might be more in tune with the detail, the fine print, the nuts and bolts. There is no right or wrong to any personal profile, just consequences from the resulting behaviour.

Self-help to self-discovery: 30 questions to self-awareness

1 To identify areas for change you first need to identify your own profile, so take some time to complete the following questionnaire.

2 Think of the set of questions from a specific viewpoint; for example, try it from a work or family viewpoint, and resist the temptation to over-think your answers.

3 This is not a psychometric test dealing with personality or career aptitude. It is simply an indicator of your preferences in a particular context.

4 An explanation of the individual traits indicated in your profile and their implications for confidence is given after you have answered it.

Personal profiler 1: 30 questions to your real self

Please answer the 30 questions on the range indicators below as honestly as you can by allocating a total of 5 points for each one, using any of the following combinations:

How to score:

If A is completely characteristic of what you would do and B is completely uncharacteristic.

If A is almost completely characteristic, but you might, on occasion, favour B.

If A is only slightly more characteristic than B.

If B is only slightly more characteristic than A.

If B is almost completely characteristic, but you might, on occasion, favour A.

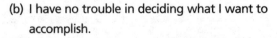

If B is completely characteristic of what you would do and A is completely uncharacteristic.

Note: Question 31 has a different scoring system.

Questions 1-30

1 I usually get up in the mornings to:

(a) Avoid creating a problem if I do not.

(b) Look forward to the day ahead.

2 When I want to set myself targets to aim for:

(a) I often find it difficult to decide what I want.

(b) I have no trouble in deciding what I want to accomplish.

3 In most situations:

(a) I know what I must avoid doing or do not want to happen.

(b) I often find it difficult to recognise what I should avoid.

4 I find it very motivational to:

(a) Do the things I really must do.

(b) Explore opportunities and possibilities.

5 When the 'chips are down' I have the tendency to:

(a) Take things as they come.

(b) Look for other options.

6 When I get involved in situations and activities:

(a) I would prefer to work to a set plan of action.

(b) I enjoy considering new procedures and alternatives.

7 I would describe myself as:

(a) Sensitive.

(b) Cool.

8 When watching a movie I am more influenced by a style that is:

(a) Exciting, dynamic, absorbing and enthusiastic.

(b) Well structured, logical, rational and factual.

9 I would be more comfortable in a job that requires:

(a) Sustained empathy and emotional involvement.

(b) Someone who can handle tough situations calmly without getting carried away by emotions.

10 I am good at:

(a) Getting the job done.

(b) Analysing and understanding the situation.

11 Which set of words would you tend to use?

(a) Go for it; just do it; why wait; right now.

(b) Give it some thought; consider this; understand; look before you leap.

12 I would rather be:

(a) An entrepreneur.

(b) A researcher.

13 When given a big task to do, I would much prefer to:

(a) Break it down into smaller, more manageable tasks.

(b) Concentrate on the overall direction of the task.

14 If interrupted when explaining something to another person, I would prefer to:

(a) Go back to the beginning and start again.

(b) Start where I left off and move forward.

15 When asked to decide how to do something, I would prefer to start:

(a) By establishing all the facts I need to know before making any decisions.

(b) By looking at the 'big picture' first to help me put the facts in their proper places.

16 If someone else tries to tell me what they think I should do:

(a) I would resist and use my own judgement.

(b) I would welcome their opinions and take their ideas into full consideration.

17 When I have completed a task successfully:

(a) I do not need anybody else to tell me that I have done well.

(b) I really appreciate other people confirming that the task was well done.

18 If I have got to make an important decision, I would much prefer:

(a) To work it out for myself, without outside interference.

(b) Find out the best course of action by asking other people what I should do.

19 When you feel that it is time to recharge your batteries do you prefer to be:

(a) Alone.

(b) With people.

20 When you are working on a project are you more effective if you:

(a) Have sole responsibility for the project.

(b) Share responsibility with others.

21 If you are working on your own in an office would you concentrate better by:

(a) Keeping the door closed to avoid distractions.

(b) Allowing occasional interruptions to give you a break and help you re-focus.

22 When you have a choice over the type of work you do, do you prefer:

(a) Tasks that are similar to what you have done before.

(b) Tasks that are completely new to you.

23 If you were to take a job with a different company, which would you enjoy the most:

(a) A company with well-established processes and methods.

(b) A company where the requirements and methods are frequently changing.

24 Which set of words have most appeal to you:

(a) Consistent – alike – identical – standard – adjacent.

(b) Unique – changing – new – different – opposite.

25 If you were to arrive 15 minutes late to a meeting how would you act:

(a) Be tough on yourself for not being punctual.

(b) Apologise and forget it.

26 **Which of the following describes your general behaviour:**

(a) Always on time for appointments, often arriving with time to spare.

(b) Often rushing from A to B to avoid being late.

27 **Do you tend to work mostly:**

(a) To a predefined and set plan.

(b) By responding to situations as they arise.

28 **When, as a member of a team, you have to make a quick decision, are you more likely to:**

A	B

(a) Decide what's best using your own judgement.

(b) Involve others and take their views into consideration.

29 **Which of the following do you consider to be the most important way for you to organise work:**

A	B

(a) To fit in with your requirements first, then to meet the needs of others.

(b) To fit the requirements of other people, and to meet your needs as a secondary consideration.

30 **What is most important to you as a member of a work group:**

A	B

(a) Having things go the way you planned.

(b) Helping meet the needs of other group members.

31 Which of the following is most likely to influence your decision to accept a new job?

(Rank the items below in order of preference from 1–5, where 1 = least influence and 5 = most influence)

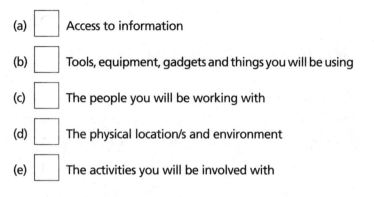

(a) ☐ Access to information

(b) ☐ Tools, equipment, gadgets and things you will be using

(c) ☐ The people you will be working with

(d) ☐ The physical location/s and environment

(e) ☐ The activities you will be involved with

How to score

Add up the A and B scores for each set of three questions (1, 2, 3; 4, 5, 6, etc.). The score for each set (A and B) adds up to 15.

Group of questions		A	B
1, 2, 3	Motivational direction		
4, 5, 6	Procedures/Options		
7, 8, 9	Response (feeling/thinking)		
10, 11, 12	Doing/considering		
13, 14, 15	Chunk size		
16, 17, 18	Frame of reference		
19, 20, 21	Working proximity		
22, 23, 24	Sameness/difference		
25, 26, 27	Through time/in time		
28, 29, 30	Self/others		

Personal profiler 2: Turning the scores into character traits

You can now establish your personal profile by shading in your total A and B scores on the range indicators below, and the bar for question 31.

MOTIVATIONAL DIRECTION (Questions 1, 2, 3)

Towards people are driven by goals, new challenges and objectives. They may appear confident to **away from** people who are motivated to avoid unpleasantness, danger and risk.

PROCEDURES/OPTIONS (Questions 4, 5, 6)

Procedural people are great for getting things done – all they need is a procedure and they will follow it. They may appear confident to **options** people because they are not distracted by alternative ways of doing things. What they do not see, however, is the stress caused by the introduction of alternative ways of doing things, which the **options** people are happy to explore.

RESPONSE (Questions 7, 8, 9)

Thinking people may appear more confident to **feeling** people because they are rational and logical. However, inside they may be wishing they could associate with the feeling and passion that comes so naturally to the **feeling** person or their perception could be that a **feeling** person does not have any confidence and gets too emotionally involved.

DOING/CONSIDERING (Questions 10, 11, 12)

Someone who is constantly on the go and doing things may appear very confident to someone who prefers to sit back and consider a little more. Conversely someone who has the patience to take time to consider the implications and plan may appear more confident to the **doer**.

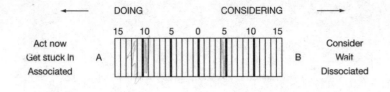

CHUNK SIZE (Questions 13, 14, 15)

A person who talks in big picture language about concepts and ideas may appear confident to the person who becomes frustrated by lack of detail. Conversely the **big picture** or **global** person may have his confidence challenged when asked for more detail.

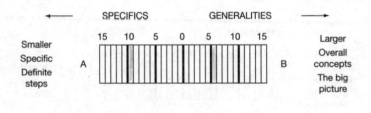

FRAME OF REFERENCE (Questions 16, 17, 18)

These patterns determine the source of feedback we use to judge our actions. The feedback can come from two places, either external, i.e. from other people, or from internal thoughts and feelings. An internally referenced person may create the illusion of inner confidence compared to someone who is constantly asking for feedback from others.

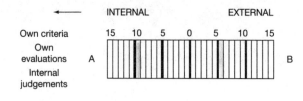

WORKING PROXIMITY (Questions 19, 20, 21)

This identifies whether a person has a preference to work alone or with others. A person who prefers to work alone may appear to lack confidence to someone who wants to be in the centre of things. Conversely someone who needs people around them all the time may see an independent person who can act alone as very confident.

SAMENESS/DIFFERENCE (Questions 22, 23, 24)

Someone who prefers sameness may become stressed by too much change. However, doing things the same way repeatedly can appear as confidence to someone who is always seeking new and different ways to do things. Taking on new and different challenges can appear like confidence to the person who prefers sameness.

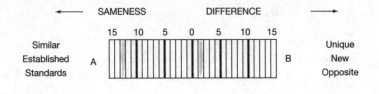

SAMENESS · DIFFERENCE

15 10 5 0 5 10 15

Similar · Established · Standards · A · B · Unique · New · Opposite

THROUGH-TIME/IN-TIME (Questions 25, 26, 27)

Being well organised and structured can be construed as confidence to the **in-time** person who is perpetually trying to catch up with themselves and is distracted by what is happening in the moment. However, to a **through-time** person, the **in-time** person who can walk into a meeting 10 minutes late without causing himself stress can appear very confident.

SELF/OTHERS (Questions 28, 29, 30)

To a self-oriented person someone who is concerned about others may appear to be a worrier and therefore lacking in confidence.

FOCUS OF INTEREST (Question 31)

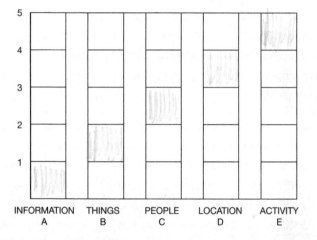

Focus/Primary interest

We know from everyday contact with our friends and colleagues that people have specific interests in life. What we often do not recognise is the larger pattern of interests, or the category. At that level you may notice how a person filters for certain categories of interest. Some people may filter for only one.

There are five general categories of interests that we filter:

1   **Things-focused people** will appear to be very knowledgeable and talk with authority about gadgets, technology, machinery, fashions, belongings, etc. which may appear as confidence to those who do not have this focus of interest.

2   **Places-focused people** will make choices in life based on location characteristics such as climate, view, convenience, travel distance and aesthetics. The office location and environment are extremely important factors in their job satisfaction. When arranging a meeting, the location will be as important as the agenda. Location-focused people will appear to be very knowledgeable and talk freely about the places they have visited and the environments they find themselves in, which may appear as confidence to those who do not have this focus of interest.

3   **People-focused people** have a strong interest in relationships of all kinds, and this will cause them to remember a variety of information about others – birthdays, children's names, team members' names, what you were doing five years ago when you last met, and so on. They will also sound knowledgeable and talk freely about people they have seen, met, know, read about and this may appear as confidence to those who do not have this focus of interest.

4   **Information-focused people** will seek out sources of information including societies, journals, libraries, Internet sites and news services. They are likely to have large stores of books and other reference media in their office and at home. Their ability to recall facts and figures can be very unnerving to those who do not have this focus of interest.

5   **Action-oriented lifestyles** distinguish activity-focused people. They are always on the move and have a great activity content in their conversations. These people will appear to be very active and talk freely about the things they have done, sports they are involved in and mountains they have climbed, which

may appear as confidence to those who do not have this focus of interest.

Personal profiler: Combinations of character traits and what they mean

Combinations of these traits can create an even greater illusion of both confidence and lack of it. To illustrate we have exaggerated some of these combinations and given them names as follows.

Blagger
A combination of moving towards and generalities.

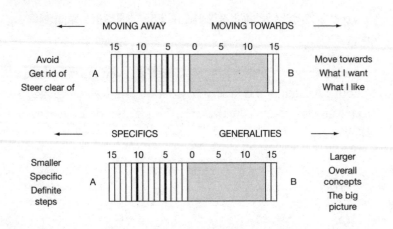

The blagger is likely to be advocating his ideas and concepts in very broad terms to anyone who will listen, probably in a highly excitable fashion.

Key question – 'Does he ever put any detail around his ideas before he moves on to the next one?'

Sergeant major
A combination of internal reference and procedure.

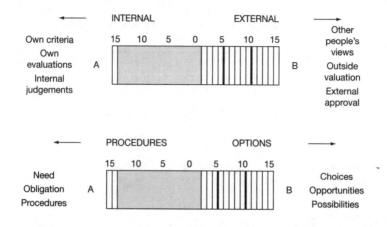

The sergeant major knows instinctively that what he is doing is right without referring to others and has a procedure for seeing it through.

Key question – 'If he had consulted others, would he have found a better way of doing it?'

Microscope
A combination of specifics and external reference.

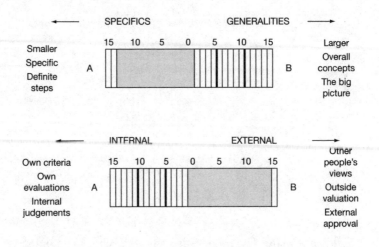

	SPECIFICS	GENERALITIES	
←		→	

Smaller
Specific
Definite
steps

A   15   10   5   0   5   10   15   B

Larger
Overall
concepts
The big
picture

	INTERNAL	EXTERNAL	
←		→	

Own criteria
Own
evaluations
Internal
judgements

A   15   10   5   0   5   10   15   B

Other
people's
views
Outside
valuation
External
approval

The microscope does not let anything past him – he never makes a mistake because he is so busy checking all the detail against any kind of measure he feels is appropriate. He may not know when 'enough data is enough' and may feel there is always more information 'out there'.

Key question – 'Is so much detail really necessary and is he hindering progress?'

Other combinations of character

Station master

A combination of procedure and through-time.

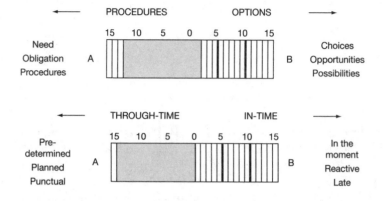

The station master gets things done accurately and on time. A well thought-through timetable keeps him on track. Time itself is as, or maybe more, important than what you do with it. There is only one time at which the train can leave and being early or late is unthinkable.

Key question – 'What happens when things do not go according to plan?'

Idealist
A combination of generalities and procedure.

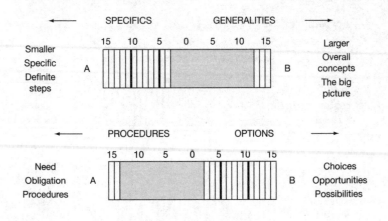

The idealist sees only one way of doing something and is not distracted from his global plans by alternative ideas and suggestions.

Key question – 'Are his ideas still relevant and universally acceptable?'

Gunslinger
A combination of doing and internal reference.

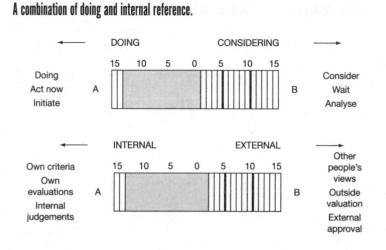

The gunslinger knows instinctively what to do without referring to others and just gets on with it – shooting from the hip.

Key question – 'Have all the implications of his actions been taken into consideration?'

Downer
A combination of away from and external reference.

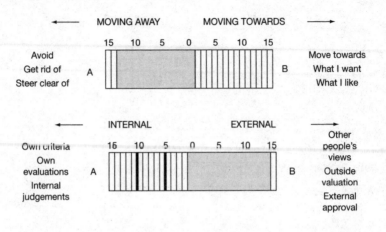

This person will inevitably lack confidence because he spends his time looking for negative feedback, and he is likely to construct a negative from any set of circumstances.

Key question – 'What positive feedback is he missing whilst looking for negative evidence?'

Procrastinator
A combination of options and considering.

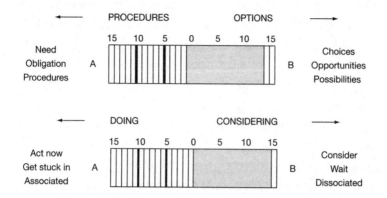

This person will have trouble making the simplest decisions because of the amount of time taken considering all the options. It's as though the person gets stuck in 'thinking mode' and only takes action under stress when there is immediate pain or reward involved.

Key question – 'How do you know when it's time to stop thinking of all the possibilities and take action?'

Is ignorance bliss when it comes to confidence?

Nobel-prize winning author Pearl S. Buck once said that, 'The young don't know enough to be prudent and therefore they attempt the impossible and achieve it'. It is the, 'If I'd known I wouldn't have tried' scenario. You could say that the blagger, the sergeant major, and the rest are all acting from a position of 'ignorance is bliss'. They are either consciously or unconsciously choosing to ignore something in order to demonstrate their so-called confidence. The blagger ignores the detail, the sergeant major ignores, or is unaware of, alternative ways of doing things and other people's opinions and so on.

Alternatively you could argue that a lack of information creates a lack of confidence. Without a procedure and a plan the station

master would not be able to continue to operate. What happens to the blagger when he or she is faced with detail? Do they become stressed and lose confidence? Similarly does the sergeant major lose his confidence when asked to choose between alternatives?

"People with true confidence have the most flexibility of behaviour."

Exercise: Use your profiler to increase confidence

People with true confidence have the most flexibility of behaviour.

In terms of the personal profiler this means you would have scored 8/7 or 7/8: effectively it is the centre point between the two extremes of each pair of profiles on the continuum. This means that you have the flexibility to behave confidently on both sides of the range indicator.

Step 1. If you want to increase your flexibility and therefore your confidence, select the personal profiles in which you have scored 9 or more. (These are the ones where you are extreme in one direction and therefore weak in the other direction.)

Step 2. Focus on one of these and ask yourself the following questions:

- What impact does this have on my behaviour and my relationships?
- How do people with the opposite patterns view me?
- What would happen if I 'acted' the opposite for a while?
- What part do these patterns play in my levels of confidence?

Step 3. Spend some time consciously behaving at the opposite end of your range indicators and notice the difference. A key way to do this is to 'model' yourself on someone who has achieved what you want to achieve but you are struggling to do it (perhaps through self-imposed limitations). Go up to them and ask them how they did it, spend 10 minutes in their company, then you will have a strategy for modelling a mental state and mental attitude as well as probably getting some practical advice too.

- Do people behave differently towards you?
- What impact, if any, does it have on your level of confidence?
- Revisit the positive illusion exercise (number 2 in Chapter 1) and imagine yourself behaving in this new way before you begin.

NLP TRIGGER

YOU ARE IN CHARGE OF YOUR MIND AND THEREFORE YOUR RESULTS

- Everything you do begins with one thought.

- This thought attracts other similar thoughts, and leads to your behaviour.

- By taking responsibility for the way you are thinking you can take control of your behaviour.

- If you want to be confident you must think confidently.

- To begin thinking differently you must accept the responsibility for personal change.

03

Believe in yourself

"You have to expect things of yourself before you can do them."

Michael Jordan, the greatest basketball player of all time

What you have discovered so far

- Self-awareness is the first stepping stone to building self confidence.
- How to discover yourself – your true self – through a personal profiler, 31-question, self-test programme.
- Your personal profiler and your beliefs play a major part in determining your levels of confidence.

What you are going to discover

- How to break the habit of assumptions and misguided illusions.
- How you form beliefs.
- How to build up your self-belief.

Barriers to self-belief

We all carry around beliefs that have become habitual ways of thinking: these can either limit us or help us depending on how we embed that belief. Here is a typical self-imposed illusion that is misplaced and damaging.

Case study: A matter of degrees

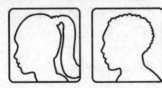

Sally Davies and Bob Gordon do excellent jobs and are in middle management in an international travel organisation. They are not at senior level yet, but they are capable, valued people well respected for their commitment and ability to get things done. Yet independently they feel lacking in confidence because they do not have a university degree. They both habitually compare themselves with colleagues who have university degrees and select their own negative experiences as evidence that they could do better if they had one.

What Sally and Bob fail to see is that people with degrees make just as many mistakes and have just as many negative experiences, but they link them to something other than a lack of a qualification – something that has just as much impact on their confidence, but that Sally and Bob are either unaware of or have chosen to ignore. What they are doing in their minds to hinder their levels of confidence is not unique to them.

"Are you influenced more by other people's beliefs than your own true experience?"

The power of belief over experience

It is easy to see how beliefs around education are formed in a society that consistently reminds us that 'education is everything' and 'you cannot get a good job without a degree'. What is interesting is that, even when you meet someone who has done well for themselves without a degree and therefore proves the belief to be invalid, the belief stays alive and current because so many other people believe it. So you are influenced more by other people's beliefs than your own true experience. Such is the power of belief and the immense impact your beliefs have on your confidence levels.

We are not suggesting that education is unnecessary, rather that a lack of education (or lack of the appropriate education) should not be used as a comparison with others, and as an excuse for things not working out, or being a disadvantage. It is equally compelling that many highly educated people, many academics, are so caught up in their intellectual prowess that they have difficulty breaking out of their thinking mode to take action about anything tangible or practical.

The business world has many high-profile examples of street-wise individuals with a basic education becoming successful by applying what they learnt about people and life. As Mark Twain said, 'I have never let my schooling interfere with my education.'

Richard Branson, founder of the Virgin global brand, said of his biggest motivation, 'I just keep challenging myself. I see life almost like one long university education that I never had – every day I'm learning something new.'

Jamie Oliver left school at 16 to enrol in a catering college; John Madejski is a self-made magnate worth £350 million, 'I never passed an exam ... I put my success down to going to the university of life; Bill Gates of Microsoft and Michael Dell both dropped out of university to pursue the 'university of life' and start up alone in business, as did Gordon Ramsay, Simon Cowell and the late Dame Anita Roddick.

A survey of small business bosses carried out by YouGov on behalf of Barclays Local Business Banking in May 2007 revealed that only 11 per cent believe that having a good education is crucial to being a success in business (and less than half actually had a degree). So the argument that educational qualifications are essential to business success are just as misguided.

Here is another example of self-imposed limitations kept alive despite evidence to the contrary but nevertheless having an impact on confidence.

Case study: Just because someone tells you so, does not make it so

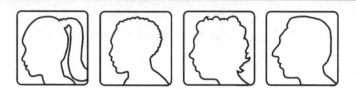

Tara Uren had a role as a customer service manager in which she was highly capable: however, she had a limiting belief that she was 'hopeless at English'. She regularly wrote highly sensitive letters to customers that were entirely off her own bat and yet she continued to believe that she was 'hopeless at English' so much so that she lacked the confidence to take part in an exercise involving anything to do with the structure of language.

Her belief originated from an English teacher at school who had encouraged Tara to become an accountant (a career she loathed) because her English was poor.

"Beware the beliefs that others try to force upon you."

Case study: 'He or she is more experienced'

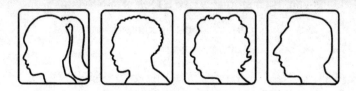

Peter Brook, the famous theatre director, in his wonderful book *The Open Space* speaks of established actors going to pieces in the presence of experience. During a showing of a tribute to Dame Judy

Dench well-known actors described how their knees turned to jelly and fear took over when they were first tasked with acting alongside her – until of course they got to know her as a fun-loving human being.

So what happened in these moments when confidence seemed to disappear? No one took away their acting skills – they did not suddenly become amateurs again. It is all an illusion created by a perception – and based on a belief. If you believe that you will forget how to act in the presence of a master (or an audience for that matter), then you will get what you focus on.

Beauty is but skin deep

In a highly cosmetic world of 'nip and tuck' it is easy to under-stand how some people become fixated on improving their looks. The media is constantly reminding us how imperfect we are and how, by the use of certain products, we can have the perfect skin, hair and body shape. It is no bad thing to want to look and feel good, but the reality for some people goes far beyond this. Until they achieve their 'perfect' look they become ever more dissatisfied with themselves as a person and self-esteem progressively erodes. From here it is only a small step to self-abuse.

If this is you, then stop and take a look around you.

1 Stop looking for perfect people to compare yourself with: this will feed only your dissatisfaction.

2 Begin instead to observe ordinary folk who, regardless of how they look, just seem to get on with life.

3 Notice how happy these people are, and how their confidence has nothing to do with their looks, but more about how they are connecting and engaging with people around them.

They say that beauty comes from within, and you can notice people whose physical features may suggest something far less than pretty or handsome, but because of the way they project their energy outward, they appear to attract people towards them.

The French actor Gérard Depardieu has a big nose and small eyes, normally not attractive features, yet he is a heartthrob to women around the world because he projects something from deeper inside. Look at pictures of other famous people such as Danny DeVito who is small and chubby, Shane MacGowan of the Irish rock group The Pogues and his terrible teeth, Brian Adams and his acne. Ask yourself if their success is due to their looks or something else.

Test it out for yourself by looking for the opposite; people who look physically attractive, but when you get close up and listen to how they communicate, the attraction loses its power! And vice versa: overcome a reluctance to talk to someone, say at a party, who looks unappealing and yet who the more you talk with reveals a warm and engaging personality.

Excuses and illusions

Of course, you could come back at us with all kinds of excuses for the success of the people highlighted above, such as talent, privilege or luck, but you would be using excuses to justify your own lack of self-esteem. You see all these people had to:

- discover and develop their talent
- work hard to get somewhere
- focus on something more important than how they look
- focus on what they wanted to do!

When your energy is focused in on your illusion of unattractiveness it is unlikely you will put in the time and effort it takes to really make something of yourself. When you take all this into account you arrive at the conclusion that whatever illusion you are using to create your life, it is all founded on what you believe about yourself.

Where does the doubt come from?

We now know confidence can be challenged severely by the presence of a limiting belief such as:

- 'She's got a degree, she must be better than me.'
- 'If I did **that**, then I know **this** would happen.'
- 'He's reached that level in the firm, I cannot possibly ask him.' ('My suggestion will get a thumbs down').
- 'I'm no good at [insert ————* here]' – relationships*, English*, maths*, socialising*, sport*, presentations*, quizzes*, selling*, influencing*, singing* or relaxing*.
- 'I'm not attractive enough for people to like me.'

How we form limiting beliefs

We adopt limiting beliefs by:

- comparing ourselves to someone else
- looking at things and putting a meaning on them – critically a negative meaning.

That then forms a limiting belief and informs our way of thinking, which will predict and determine our behaviour.

Beliefs that get in the way of confidence

Limiting beliefs form part of everyday language and, if left unchallenged, form the basis for habitually avoiding unpleasant or difficult scenarios. The nature of any belief is such that once formed it attracts evidence to support it and deletes anything to the contrary. It may be a tenuous belief but we like to defend our beliefs and will go to great lengths to do so.

The sad thing is that it takes only one experience, such as a dinner party that did not go as well, for the belief 'I'm no good at dinner parties' to be formed, confidence to be knocked and future dinner parties to be avoided at all cost.

Weighing your beliefs against your values

To set about changing beliefs that are getting in the way of confidence you need to explore your values. In other words – is what you would dearly love to be able to achieve **important** enough to you?

This can be a bit of a chicken and egg type question because you may tell yourself things are not important because you do not believe you can achieve them. They get put on the back burner whilst you continue to focus on the things you believe you can achieve. Often such things may never be considered again.

"Eliminating negative beliefs and creating a new more empowering illusion around things that are important to you is key to increasing your confidence."

When something becomes important in your mind, and belief is built in place around its achievability – this is the point at which you will look for the skills and opportunities to practise. For example, Pat McCoy disliked science at school and avoided anything to do with biology, physics and chemistry until she developed a value around health and nutrition. Suddenly the value was much stronger than her belief that she was no good at science and she was able to successfully pass her exams in nutrition.

So eliminating negative beliefs and creating a new more empowering illusion around things that are important to you is key to increasing your confidence. Here's an exercise to do just that.

Exercise: Shake off negative beliefs (replace with an empowering belief)

Use this exercise to shake your negative illusion and replace it with a more empowering one.

Step 1. Take a pad of sticky notes and find a quiet place where you can relax and let your mind flow freely.

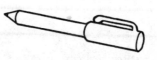

Step 2. Make sure you have a blank wall on which to stick your notes, put on some background music and begin to write.

Step 3. Create a sticky note for all the things you have told yourself you do not have the confidence to do. It does not matter whether they are small things or large, life-changing things. As you complete each sticky note place it on the wall above eye level but in no particular order. When you think you have finished leave the room and do something else to distract your mind.

Step 4. Return after a while and now make sense of your notes. Ask yourself:

'If in five years' time I have not achieved this, how will I feel?'

If the answer is indifferent then it probably is not important to you and you can put the note to one side.

To aid this 'pruning' process, and highlight a few things that you would dearly like to achieve – if only you had the confidence – ask yourself:

'What would achieving this particular thing get for me?'

You may find that the answers to this question tie back to your 'personal profile' (see page 34).

Step 5. Now, with your shortlist, take each sticky note in turn and ask yourself:

'What do I believe about my ability to achieve this?'

Write down any thoughts on new sticky notes that limit or obstruct your beliefs in achieving this. For example, you may have written, 'Do a parachute jump,' but your sticky note belief might say, 'I won't be able to breathe,' or 'My parachute won't open.'

Step 6. Challenge each negative belief with a series of questions and use them to challenge any limiting belief you catch yourself saying.

- Where does this belief originate from?
- Where is the evidence to support this belief?
- Where is the evidence to the contrary?
- What will happen if I continue to hold this belief?
- What could happen if I believed the opposite?
- In what way is this belief ridiculous?
- What would be a better, more empowering belief to have?

Getting the right 'tone of voice'

■ State your new belief in a positive tone of voice and make it as forceful as you can.

To help you get used to the idea of 'tone' try these phrases putting emphasis on the highlighted word each time you recite them aloud. Say them slowly, exaggerate the intonation, especially at the end (up or down), and turn up the volume!

1 'I am going to feel really good today whatever happens'

2 'I **AM** going to feel really good today whatever happens'

3 'I am **GOING** to feel really good today whatever happens'

4 'I am going to **FEEL** really good today whatever happens'

5 'I am going to feel **REALLY** good today whatever happens'

6 'I am going to feel really **GOOD** today whatever happens'

7 'I am going to feel really good **TODAY** whatever happens'

8 'I am going to feel really good today **WHATEVER** happens'

9 'I am going to feel really good today whatever **HAPPENS**'

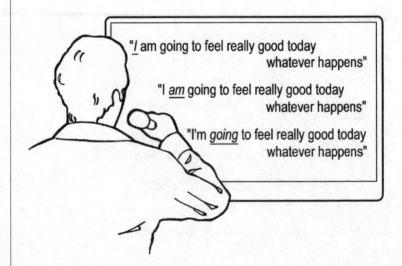

- Use a tone of voice that motivates and encourages you to get up and do something.

- If it helps, imagine the tone of someone with a highly distinctive, forceful and positive voice such as James Bond (Daniel Craig, Sean Connery or Roger Moore), actor Jim Carrey, presenter Jeremy Paxman, even Arnold Schwarzenegger (as Governor of California or as *Terminator!*).

- Just to feel the negative tone try saying the phrase in the voice of comedians Jack Dee or Bill Murray or the TV character David Brent or radio panellist Clement Freud.

- Practise saying the new belief to yourself until it becomes automatic.

- Remember that everything you say to yourself – internally with an inner voice or using your external voice – is like a command you are embedding more deeply into your character and personality.

With confidence there is no limit to achieving your goals

Now begin to imagine for a moment, if confidence was not an issue, just what you would do. Just how much you could achieve?

- How many eloquent presentations could you give?

- How many fabulous dinner parties could you throw?

- How many people could you influence?

- How many daring decisions could you make?

- How much flirting could you do?

- What talent could you develop?

- Would you end a dysfunctional relationship, change your job or even your career?

- How would you start a relationship with someone new, move house, end a contract, make a difficult phone call?
- How might you treat your children any differently?
- How might you do something out of character, start a business, take up a new sport, or play a musical instrument?

NLP TRIGGER

WHATEVER YOU BELIEVE YOU WILL DEFEND

- The nature of any belief is that once you adopt it you will tend to defend it and seek evidence to hold it to be true. This applies equally to religion, spirituality and beliefs about yourself and your abilities.

- So if you believe you **cannot**, then you will make sure that you never succeed. If you believe you are timid and shy you will find plenty of evidence to keep the belief alive. If you believe Jack is lazy you will convince yourself this is true.

- But if you believe you **can**, you will look for ways to succeed. So why not use this incredible process to defend empowering, confidence-building beliefs? You can do this – if you believe it – and your belief will soon begin to change the way you feel about yourself and what you are truly capable of.

■ Believe in yourself – use empowering beliefs – engage and tell yourself with your voice tone – and build your confidence further.

04

Stay on the field, 'Keep the shutters open'

"Life is full of obstacle illusions."

Grant Frazier, author

What you have discovered so far

- How to build up an awareness of yourself.

- Understanding what confidence is, and what it is not.

- How your personal values, your 'profiles' (in NLP speak 'metaprogrammes') and beliefs underpin all your behaviour and create your level of confidence in any particular scenario.

What you are going to discover

- How to decide what to do, and what not to do, where to go and where not to go.

- How to invite more of life to engage with you.

- How the things you used to perceive as obstacles will become small speed bumps in the road – unavoidable, but insignificant in the grander scheme of things.

- Living your life in this way requires you to stay 'on the field of play' for much longer periods of time. This means staying connected with people and not withdrawing inside your head when things get tough out there.

When somebody lacks confidence they tend to withdraw within themselves. You can put your attention in only one of two places:

1 **'Out there'** – so you are watching and listening to what people are saying and responding in kind.

2 **'In here'** – all your communication is directed to internal dialogue, 'towards me' because you feel you have nothing to say. You may be there physically, with associates, colleagues, family or friends, but you have 'left the field', 'closed down' with a 'what-is-the-point?' attitude, and gone inside your head.

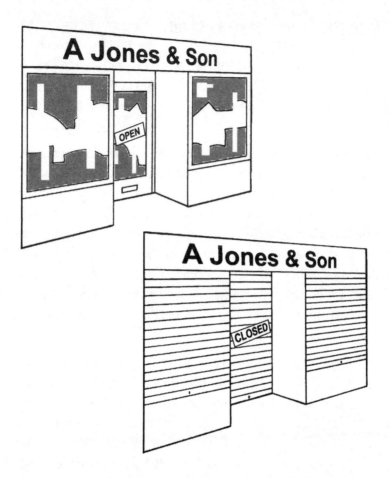

This can be bound up with a feeling of low self-esteem; that is a deep lack of self-confidence and a tendency to create very negative illusions about 'self'. You are totally focused on yourself all the time, and whilst you are focusing on you, you are not focusing on the people around you. This obsession with self is a kind of self-indulgence.

The limitations of asking 'Why?'

People who continually ask the question 'Why?' are removing themselves from the field of play and keeping their self-esteem at a low ebb. How? Well, this question will eventually drive you crazy because there are as many answers as can be imagined, each one creating yet further illusions. From toddlerdom through teenager to one's twenties asking 'Why?' becomes a default mechanism of our formative years and very soon a dangerous habit.

For example, think back to your earliest childhood memories: can you remember seeing something in a shop window and asking for it? 'Will you buy me those sweets?' Maybe your parents replied, 'No, it's dinner time very soon.' You probably responded with, 'But why?' No matter how much logic parents throw at toddlers it never seems like logic as the feelings of desire override all answers – except the one the toddler wants to hear. So we grow up without a satisfactory answer to 'Why?' and this continues as we go through puberty and begin to ponder the idea of mortality.

Then you are grown up and at work. Your bosses and colleagues do all kinds of things to make life difficult for you and again you are asking why: 'Why is John so lazy?' 'Why doesn't my boss

notice me?' 'Why do I have to go to this boring meeting every week?' 'Why can't I seem to connect with these people?' 'Why does my boss look at me in that odd way?' And so on. And you still have not learned that it rarely brings you a satisfactory answer.

"Whichever way **why?** is directed, it always comes back to make you feel inadequate in some way, and so the downward spiral of low self-esteem continues."

Asking 'Why?' leads to feelings of inadequacy

People who have low self-esteem often ask 'Why?' questions of themselves like the ones above. They can be directed as follows:

1 inward, as with, 'Why don't I have any confidence?' or

2 outward in the form of blaming, which is usually laced with anger, as in, 'Why won't they listen to me?'

Whichever way it is directed, it always comes back to make you feel inadequate in some way, and so the downward spiral of low self-esteem continues.

Asking 'Why?' is illusory

A more fundamental problem with asking 'Why?' is that it assumes the statement it is responding to is actually true or valid. So if you say, 'Why doesn't my boss notice me?' there is an assumption that he does not, and this may be a gigantic illusion. Once you ask 'Why?' you begin to build the illusion you have chosen to believe.

So change the question

Whenever you find yourself in an unsatisfactory situation (or with an uncomfortable feeling) and you ask a 'Why' question, bite your tongue and rephrase it with a 'What' or 'How' question. These questions will keep you focused on real observable actions and steer you away from your negative illusion. For example, change 'Why don't I have any confidence?' (your negative illusion – merely looking for justification for how you feel, and any answer will do), to 'How am I going to become more confident?' (building a positive illusion – encouraging you to explore a way to become confident).

Confidence and self-esteem are inextricably linked. This also means that if you consider yourself to have low self-esteem the techniques used to develop confidence will also build your self-esteem.

Exercise: From awareness to action

From the self-awareness you have so far, you can take the short step to using some NLP techniques to create the kind of confidence that is transferable to any situation. So let us take a quick review before considering the conditions that need to be in place for this to happen.

Tick the box if you agree with the following:

1 Confidence is a general attitude of mind with positive feelings that can be applied to any situation. ☐

2 Familiarity is often mistaken for confidence. ☐

3 True confidence is only ever tested in unfamiliar territory. ☐

4 Comparison is a useful way of noticing what other people do to get results. ☐

5 Judging a person's actions will block your attempts to be more confident. ☐

6 Judging yourself will also block your attempts to be more confident. ☐

7 Your metaprogramme profile and your personal values will influence where you direct your attention and where you do not. ☐

8 What you believe will determine what you are prepared to do to become confident. ☐

9 Asking 'Why?' will keep you where you are. Asking 'What?' and 'How?' will help you to move to a more confident position.

You may agree with our checklist 1–9 but there is another crucial factor – number 10 – that is not there – conquering fear

No fear

There is a video clip on Google showing a boy called Aaron Fotheringham learning to perform stunts in his wheelchair. The video shows his early attempts where he fell often, through to the first ever 360° flip performed in a wheelchair, and on to even more advanced and amazing techniques. As you watch this video (www.youtube.com/watch?v=A_Z7rV7kKnI or search on You Tube for Aaron Fotheringham) you will notice how Aaron approaches every new stunt with no hesitation whatsoever. Call it confidence if you must, but notice **how he seems confident from the outset to learn and have a go**, and the more he attempts the more quickly his ability grows. You might think his confidence is growing, but it appears he had plenty of confidence even before he tried his very first stunt. Watch it and make up your own mind.

It may be an extreme example but it makes the point. Compare the confidence of Aaron Fotheringham to your everyday reality.

We have lost count of the many people who have said that they fear an upcoming presentation. Our response is usually the same, 'What preparation have you done?' Most reply, 'Very little – I put it together the day before.'

"All you need to take the first step is enough confidence to motivate yourself into wanting to succeed."

You need to be on the field to have an impact on the field

When you see a confident speaker what you do not see are the many hours, days and weeks of practice to hone their skill and rehearse their topic. You also do not see them carefully studying and copying the techniques of other speakers they admire, but they do. The same goes for any performance, whether on stage, a track, a sportsfield, at a party, in a meeting, with a project or with a relationship. Yet still, so many people hope to perform well without putting in the effort. Hope achieves very little without skill and attitude.

When a person fears social interaction the last thing they do is to see how many parties they can get invited to. Yet this is exactly what they ought to be doing – to gain experience and practice – to rehearse. This is how you become proficient at anything. Whether it is socialising, presenting, starting a business or indeed anything – at some point you have to launch yourself into it and start making mistakes – just like Aaron

Fotheringham. You need to be on the field to have an impact on the field. All you need to take the first step is enough confidence to motivate yourself into wanting to succeed.

Giving it your best shot

Giving a presentation at work, or a speech at a social gathering, is exposing you to being perceived, judged and valued by your audience – and surely you want to make the right impression? So does it not make sense to give it your best shot? Why then are there so many people who just do not see things this way?

The same 'best shot' applies just as much to being confident in relationships, to pursuing a lifelong ambition, to turning a hobby into a business, to finding fulfilling work and to generally feeling good about yourself, regardless of what is going on around you.

Feelings get in the way

Yet if practice is all there is to it, building confidence would not be such an apparent struggle. The problem is that feelings get in the way. So you end up saying things like, 'I'm just not a confident person,' and thus taking a bad feeling from one area and generalising it in all areas. Then no matter how much you practise, you are already expecting to fail. If it were not for feelings you would be able to logically become more confident at everything. But feelings keep getting in the way. It is unlikely that Aaron Fotheringham ever told himself he was not a confident boy.

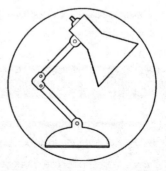

"One of the first requirements for confidence is that there is something worthwhile to aim for."

The need for a desire, want or aspiration

To live and work without a desire or aspiration is like joining a cruise liner and not caring where you are sailing to. You are not at the helm and have no control over your destination. So you spend your time reacting to other people and events and hope for something good.

One of the first requirements for confidence is that there is something worthwhile to aim for.

How to go about creating an aspiration

What do you value to bring you 'onto the field' and to have a gameplan?

1 It could be something just for you, or for someone else.

2 Whatever you choose it must be important enough for you to put time and effort into the achievement.

3 Just pick one thing to begin with. (There are so many choices these days that it is easy to want to do too many things and you will never get around to doing any one thing particularly well.)

4 You may already have a strong aspiration, or it may be something you have rarely experienced. It does not matter so long as you just find something that stirs up a positive energy whenever you think about having achieved it.

5 The way to build an aspiration is to use your imagination to create strong, colourful mental images of what you want to be confident at.

Watching others

If you were to spend some time around people who consistently achieve things – and that in itself is a worthwhile aspiration – you would notice how driven and focused they seem to be.

People with drive and focus:

- do not waste time with unproductive activities
- make every minute of the day count towards achieving something of value – and often that value is having a good time!
- know what to ignore and what to focus on.

This comes from a deep desire, or aspiration, to have an impact somewhere, and everything they do seems to have some link to this aspiration.

Exercise: To create an aspiration

Warm up

So let us try to simply 'stay in the field' as a warm up.

1 Select one activity from the exercise in Chapter 3 in which you really do want to be more confident.

2 Take your time and think of one thing that, if you were to approach it with supreme confidence, would have a positive impact for you.

3 As you think about this activity notice how you feel and how motivated you are to do something about it and get stuck in.

Now it is time to get stuck in.

The exercise

1 Choose a situation in which you would like to be confident.

2 Create an image of yourself approaching this situation with absolute rock solid confidence. If your mental image is not very

bright raise your eyes to a point above the horizon and notice how the picture suddenly brightens up. You can do this with eyes closed if this makes it easier for you to visualise, and remember to keep your images projected above the horizon line.

3 Run a movie in your mind ending in a positive result, and then capture one frame of your movie that shows you being your most confident.

4 Now bring this image a little closer and brighten it even more.

5 At the same time use a confident tone of voice to add to the motivation with words like, 'OK, time to make this happen.' Say these words to yourself with internal dialogue. As you do this notice how positive feelings become stronger and get used to this feeling as it will form part of your motivation to get up and make a difference.

Becoming 'associated'

Being associated means having all your senses tuned in to noticing and observing what is happening as you pursue your achievement in your mind's eye. We think in pictures, so use your images in a positive way. Your awareness of your aspiration

is heightened along with your emotional connection. In such a state you are much less likely to become distracted with negative feelings and get thrown off the field. Being associated is the state you require for getting things done.

"You want to be fully associated with all your senses when you are getting things done that are important to you."

Danger: attention wavering

Have you ever had trouble finding your keys because at the moment you put them down you were thinking of something else – splitting your attention?

People often struggle to achieve things because their attention is split across too many things. If you share 100 per cent of your attention at any one moment equally across three ongoing tasks, then each will receive only 33 per cent of your attention. This is common sense, and also common practice.

The ability to do one thing well, like driving a car or doing the washing up, whilst thinking about something else is a great example of how your conscious and unconscious minds cooperate. If you focus your mind on things or events that are disconnected with what you are currently doing, expect to lose and forget things (like your keys). Washing up and driving, of course, are no big deal – they are dealt with very effectively by your autopilot.

Your aspiration, however, should not be left to your autopilot – you want to keep a very conscious intention at the front of your mind. You want to be fully associating with all your senses when you are getting things done that are important to you.

Your 'associated–dissociated' control switch

On the other hand, when you want to put your mind to working out how to take the next step, then dissociate, 'unplug', and use your imagination to create the next steps in your mind's eye first.

When you are happy with your plan associate with it again – you can do this by mentally stepping into the picture – and continue to execute your plan. The secret is to be consciously switching your attention between associated and dissociated as required. Left to its own devices your attention will switch randomly from one thing to another, so that you end up being distracted much of the time. This is about taking what your mind is good at and using it more productively to take control of where you focus your attention – being off the field when you need to work things out, and quickly returning to the field of play to re-engage.

Directing your attention

Our attention does not just waver, it goes all over the place. Short attention spans are typical for many of us, as are problems with external distractions.

As part of the process of learning to improve conscious intention it helps to begin with an awareness of where your attention is at any moment in time. As we have noted already at the beginning of this chapter there are basically two places where you can direct your attention. These are as follows:

1 Inside your own head (or off the field).
2 Outside on other people and things (on the field).

'Downtime'

When you are deep in thought your attention is focused inside, and you will miss most of what goes on around you. You will notice this has happened when you are brought out of your inner world 'trance' by a raised voice saying, 'You are not listening to me, are you?' This condition is known as being in 'downtime', i.e. time spent down inside your own thoughts.

Downtime can be a very pleasant or useful frame of mind if you want to dwell on a pleasant experience you had, or to think through a plan. But downtime can also have negative implications. Ask yourself the following questions.

■ How much of your downtime is negative internal dialogue?

■ How often does your mind wander of its own volition, with no conscious intention?

"Energy flows where attention goes."

'Uptime'

The alternative direction for your attention is, of course, outward on other people and things. This is known as being in 'uptime' with all your senses open and receptive to what is going on in the space around you. A well-known saying has it: 'Energy flows where attention goes.'

In our experience, very few people seem able to sustain periods of uptime for long. You can tell when a person switches their attention from uptime to downtime by the movement of their eyes. When eyes begin to stare in a downward position you can bet the attention is inside, senses cut off to the outside world. Ask yourself the following questions.

Downtime – Eyes looking down

Uptime – Eyes looking up

■ How has your attention been since you began reading this text?

■ Did it wander off anywhere?

■ Where did it go, and how useful was it to be there?

With an awareness of uptime and downtime, you can begin to use each one with more control.

1 You decide when to be in uptime, and you decide when to be in downtime. People are generally quite good at being in downtime, but not so good at sustaining uptime.

2 If you want to improve your uptime attention then really stretch your sight and hearing so that you see and hear more.

3 Remember to suspend judgement – see how much more connected with other people you can be.

4 When you focus on someone or something you are noticing different features and layers and there is no time to have negative dialogue about yourself. The more you observe and ask questions about what you are looking at, the less you are able to focus in on 'self'. But as soon as you say 'I'm not feeling too good about myself,' your attention goes; literally you glaze over.

5 Practise staying in uptime as long as you can. The more you practise the more you will notice and the easier it will become. (See exercise – To break out of self-obsession cycle and develop curiosity, page 16.)

Masking a lack of confidence

When a person lacks confidence they may attempt to hide it from others by a variety of means.

They often disengage somewhat to avoid drawing attention to themselves. Whilst disengaging they will probably go into downtime where it feels a little safer.

From this inwardly focused position they are likely to be creating negative illusions that are draining any small amounts of confidence that might remain.

This strategy might help them avoid awkward or trying situations but it does nothing to help self-confidence, nor does it help to build rapport with people.

What is rapport?

Rapport is like an unwritten communication between people by which they understand each other. It is a sort of bond and an extremely important part in the process of developing productive and meaningful relationships and confidence. Think about your friends – you can probably say anything you like to them – joshing in familiar tones that you would not dream of using with people who are either not yet friends or who you have only just met. When you first meet someone you go through the process of getting to know them – sometimes this is very quick and sometimes it takes a while.

If you watch people who are in rapport you will find they do similar things. They perform what can be described as a dance, moving at the same time, unconsciously matching each other's body movements, general physiology, tone of voice, language patterns, and so on. Conversely, people who are lacking rapport between them can appear awkward as they mismatch each other in all these areas.

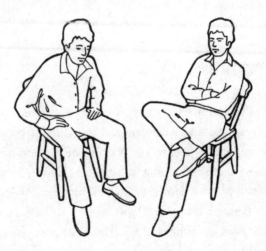

So why is this important to confidence building? People in rapport are more likely to:

- cooperate with each other
- help each other out
- work together
- play together.

You are more likely to get results from someone with whom you have rapport than someone with whom you do not.

Remember Darren in Chapter 1 (see page 12)? He had completely missed the value, along with many other people we come into contact with, of what is often referred to as small talk. Small talk is a crucial part of the rapport-building process – so much so that when we hear clients on our NLP courses using this expression we get them to imagine it as **big talk**. Without rapport, getting results – whatever they are – becomes a laborious and tedious practice.

Building rapport

The trick is to be absolutely curious to learn about the other person. If you keep going into downtime they may believe you are not interested in them, or are pre-occupied with something else. Actually the latter will be true, as you would be putting your attention on yourself – being quite self-obsessive. If you lack confidence in meeting new people and keeping conversations going try this rapport-building exercise.

Exercise: Quick 10-step exercise to build rapport

1 Find someone that you do not know, say at a supermarket, shopping mall or leisure centre.

2 Walk up to them, say 'hello'.

3 Ask them a question, preferably one that will not elicit just a 'Yes' or 'No' answer.

4 Keep your attention focused on them and observe every nuance of their facial expression, voice characteristics and body language.

5 Show an interest in what they are telling you – without comparing with yourself, and without judging.

6 Ask them something else and keep the conversation going. (People tend to prefer to talk about their own experiences more than listening to someone else, that is the point underpinning this exercise.)

7 At no point talk about yourself.

8 Keep your focus on the other person – stay in uptime – and remember to smile occasionally.

9 Notice how you feel throughout the experience.

10 Thank them for their time and trouble.

■ This exercise will help you master the technique of staying in uptime and listening carefully.

■ Once you are comfortable with this, move on to the next stage and develop the habit of remembering what has been said.

That was a wonderful remark: using memory and feedback

One of the reasons why people maintain they have poor memories is because they spend so much time focusing on themselves. As a result, they cannot concentrate on what is being said by someone else or notice body language and all the finer points that go into effective communication. If you are always inside yourself, in 'downtime', how can you possibly remember people's names? But remembering something about someone is so important, especially the next time you meet them.

If you can remember a number of key things in a conversation, however, and feed it back, people will start to change towards you. Unconsciously they will think, 'Hey, he's/she's actually interested in what I'm saying – I like this person.' They may then begin to seek out your company and, if you can then ask about something you remembered from a previous conversation, their opinion of you will really begin to soar.

Case study: Gemma

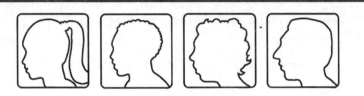

Gemma attended a training programme in London. Cruising along the motorway on a quiet Sunday morning she was enjoying the sunshine and the clear roads in her brand new sports car when she heard the sound of sirens behind her. Looking at the speedometer she realised she had gone over the limit. She pulled into the side and went through the formalities of receiving a speeding ticket. When she eventually arrived at the seminar she was about half an hour late. She made her apologies to the seminar leader and sat down. Several years later in Florida she met the seminar leader for a second time. Introducing herself she said, 'You probably don't remember me. I attended one of your programmes in London . . .' Before she could finish the sentence he said, 'Yes I do. You're the owner of that convertible – have you still got it?'

Imagine Gemma's surprise and delight that he had remembered her – he must meet literally thousands of people on his seminar circuit but in this case he was able to focus and associate on 'things'.

What sort of things are you going to remember?

The key here is to tune into the other person's focus of interest. Remember in Chapter 2 the final question in the personal profile centred on a person's main focus of interest. This is a great rapport builder. Listen carefully and they will give away what their main focus is.

They will talk about one of the following areas:

1 **People** – team, family, celebrities.

2 **Activities** – projects, tasks, sports, hobbies.

3 **Location** – where they have been, what the current surroundings are like.

4 **Information** – books, reports, websites, research.

5 **Things** – latest technology, cars, fashion, houses.

Focus on picking up these areas and use the following exercise to help you remember the key points.

Exercise: To help you remember significant facts about people

This exercise also gives you practice in consciously switching between 'uptime' and 'downtime' to maximum effect.

1 In your mind create an imaginary clipboard that you are going to use whenever you meet someone and want to remember something.

2 Be precise about its size, colour and location in relation to you.

3 Make sure your clipboard is above the horizon line and there is a place to stick notes.

4 The next time you are having a conversation with someone use the clipboard to visualise the person you are listening to, and stick up imaginary notes for key words.

5 As you create your image of the person make sure you include the physical environment you are in. This provides the context that will make it easier to remember the person at a much later time.

6 It also helps when you are meeting a number of people in quick succession, like at a meeting, seminar or party. To do this you have to momentarily, and we mean momentarily, go into downtime to visualise the person and the word and pin it up. For example, you may want to remember the person's partner's name or a key fact like 'black sports car'. You can either see the words 'sports car' or an actual picture of a sports car.

7 Continue to suspend judgement – your task is simply to accumulate and store information into your memory that you can use at a later date.

8 All the time you are doing this you are focused on something other than yourself, your thoughts and feelings.

9 Keep practising and notice how differently people respond to you.

10 Feel the impact this has on your confidence.

NLP TRIGGER

YOU CANNOT NOT COMMUNICATE

- Whatever you are doing you are giving off signals from your body language that others will interpret.

- There is no escaping communicating your state of mind through your body, breathing, voice tone, gestures and muscle tension.

- As you have decided to become a much more confident person you may as well practise giving off signals that you are confident to others.

- Begin with your state of mind and adopt both the state of mind and body that creates a feeling of confidence inside you.

Connect with others

"Always hold your head up, but be careful to keep your nose at a friendly level."
Max L. Forman, author

What you have discovered so far

■ You need to be self-aware before you can be self-confident.

■ You need to have self-belief and stop falling into the trap that you and your beliefs are worthless; it is all an illusion.

■ You have to stay engaged, curious and 'on the field of play' (not in the dug-out looking in on yourself).

What you are going to discover

■ Confidence is as much to do with being able to socialise and have meaningful relationships as anything else.

■ Wherever you want to feel confident it is a safe bet that you will need to relate confidently with other people.

■ The confidence to change your job, start a business, learn something new, start a new hobby, or simply ask for directions, will involve influencing and befriending other people in some way.

■ Posture and body language are key factors in making connections.

The saying, 'No man is an island,' reminds us that getting on in this world is easier if we can get on with other people and get them to help us. Help generally requires some kind of rapport or bond.

Projecting a confident posture

If you are going to build meaningful relationships you need to be open and take the initiative. You cannot hope that others will notice you and make the first move – you want to be proactive. You also want to project a confident body posture since a confident person is much more attractive to an onlooker than a shrinking violet. Test this for yourself by comparing soap opera actors who portray confident characters with those who portray shy characters. Which character's company would you prefer to be in?

Exercise: To project a confident posture

You need a head start: literally. A person who lacks confidence is likely to hide their feelings by making themselves small. The head droops, the shoulders slouch, and there is a general inward closing of the body. This behaviour is a natural human instinct to avoid attracting the attention of others, but it does nothing to help regain confidence. So get started by holding your head up.

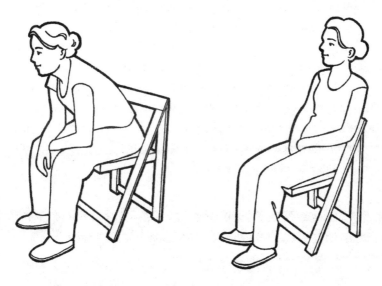

1 Every morning look in the mirror and stand up with your head up and eyes looking above the level of the horizon. How does this feel?

2 Practise this posture and use it during the day until you get used to it and it becomes a habit for you.

3 Watch other confident-looking people and notice their posture; it does not have to be stiff and rigid, rather upright and relaxed.

Approaching someone with a confident-looking posture is the first step to making new connections.

Start in the same place

The next step is to connect with conversation.

Imagining the barriers to building rapport

Think back to a time when you felt no one understood you. Maybe you were trying to get an idea across, or tell someone how you felt, but no matter what you said the response was indifference, disinterest, or even disagreement. Remember how you felt at that time, and whether you were emotionally warm or cold towards those who did not understand you. You probably did not feel very connected with them, and they may have appeared cold or arrogant. The feeling of being understood is a basic human need that creates a strong bond with the person you believe understands you.

Exercise: To help you imagine building rapport

If you are feeling daunted by going 'out there', remember that people generally have a tendency to talk about themselves rather than ask questions. So actually building rapport in this way is very easy to do.

You will be surprised at how little effort it takes to get someone talking about themselves and, as soon as they are, rapport is taking place.

1 Think of someone with whom you want to build a relationship and influence.

2 Imagine what it would be like to be this person.

3 What do you know about them? Instead of shying away, or beginning an interaction by launching into what you want, be curious to find out something about them.

4 Show an interest in who they are and what they do.

5 Listen for connections with what you want their support for and make the jump to your agenda only when you sense there is rapport between you.

Pointers to sincere rapport

■ The depth of rapport you need will depend on what you want.

■ The more you ask for, the deeper the rapport needs to be.

■ This is **not** a manipulative technique.

■ It will work only if you show a genuine and sincere interest in the person you are asking.

■ It is usually easy to tell if a person is using a technique to get something from you. The body language or tone of voice will give it away.

■ When you are truly sincere in wanting to understand someone, there is every chance that they will like you.

"When you have rapport it is a short step to ask for what you want."

Do me a favour

Some people lack the confidence to ask for help, but if you need help from another person you will be surprised at how ready to help most people are. When you have rapport it is a short step to ask for what you want. In the 'personal profile' (see Chapter 2) you can see some people have a disposition to help others, while others do not mind helping if you have built rapport first.

So just come out with what you want – be direct and to the point. Ask for the help you need and tell them why you need it. Research shows that when you use the word 'because' in your quest for help, more people are likely to respond positively to your request. One test was conducted by having someone ask to jump in front of a photocopy queue. The use of the word 'because' in their request resulted in a significantly higher number of people agreeing. Even when they said 'because I need to photocopy', those in the queue allowed the person to jump to the front.[2]

Finding a common experience to build rapport

Common experiences bond people together, even when the experience is not yours. So when one person talks about incidents like the Berlin Wall coming down, or poor communication from a call centre in India, people will be able to relate to them. Tragedies such as 9/11, or the death of Diana Princess of Wales, hold special places in a collective memory, and so form a common bond. Visiting a foreign country, going to a pop concert, a blockbuster movie, or an adventure holiday are all opportunities to find a common theme with which to create a

[2] *Yes! 50 Scientifically Proven Ways to be Persuasive* (2007), Noah J. Goldstein, Steve J. Martin and Robert B. Cialdini, Profile Books: London.

bond. When you ask questions of the other person, something in common will emerge, and you can use this to make the rapport stronger by sharing your experiences.

Exercise: To break the ice and get connected

The next time you are invited to a party, after asking the usual, 'What do you do?' or, 'Do you live around here?' questions, pretend you are a chat show host and try one of the following questions to break the ice and really get connected.

■ What kind of movies do you like?

■ What is the most memorable place you have been to?

■ Did you see the rugby/football/tennis/news/last night?

■ Do you have a favourite celebrity chef?

■ Have you ever taken an adventure holiday?

■ Do you speak any foreign languages?

■ What activity do you enjoy doing the most?

■ Did you see the final episode of xxx yesterday?

■ Which book you have read is most memorable to you?

■ Who was your best teacher at school?

■ Do you use Facebook?

■ If you had plenty of money would you buy a seat on Richard Branson's spaceship?

Remember, stay in 'chatshow host' mode and keep listening and ask follow-up questions such as:

■ What was it like?

■ How did it affect you?

■ Are you planning to do that/go there again?

■ What do you get out of it?

■ Can you imagine what it would be like?

Put that party into your diary and start to find out about people and create connections. The art of conversation is very easy once you realise that you do not have to talk about yourself. Finding out about other people is so much more fun, and learning how to socialise is a great asset. It is also a brilliant way to start creating a powerful bond so that the other person will want to cooperate with you and help you out.

Matching: talk the talk

There are some easy ways to strengthen the bond, and to speed up the rapport-building process when you need something urgently. The process is called matching, and it begins by noticing how the person is talking.

■ Pay attention to the tone and speed of their voice, and match it. You do not have to be precise, just get as close to it as you can.

■ This will unconsciously send the message that you are like them.

■ The more 'like them' you can be, the more they will find it easier to talk with you, and to trust you.

Mismatching the voice

The danger is that, if your natural voice is miles apart in terms of tone and speed, the mismatch can have the opposite effect – it may turn them off you as they feel uncomfortable talking to you. A fast talker may get frustrated and impatient listening to a slow talker, and the slow talker can feel like the fast talker is not really listening as they jump into the gaps and continue talking.

Matching: walk the walk

Now think about also matching body language, particularly gestures and movement. Taking time to watch body language is very revealing: when people are in natural rapport you often find their body language is synchronised unconsciously with one person taking the lead and the other person following – almost like a dance. Standing, sitting, leaning, bouncing on heels, folding arms, stroking the chin, and many other unconscious body movements, form part of the dance. You can match gestures and other body language in the same way as you can with the voice characteristics.

Observe other people's body gestures

Some people are very still when they are speaking, whilst others are much more animated and those people who use body movements and gestures as part of their communication have much more impact and are more memorable to others.

When there is no body language your communication is not so easy to understand, and has less impact.

Think about the people you know and the chances are those with the most animated body language will be more memorable to you. So how flexible can you be in using your body to form part of your communication?

- Watch how actors and TV presenters do this, and get ideas from them for your own style of gesturing.
- Notice also how gestures are timed to work with voice emphasis to really make a point stick.
- You can practise using confident-looking gestures such as opening the palm and fingers, and using your arms to emphasise what you say.

- Again, you do not have to be precise, just remember to match the general dance and rhythm of movement and you have another way of strengthening rapport and trust.

Mismatching the gestures

A very still person can come across as being detached to someone who is highly animated, and the animated person can come across as unstable or unbalanced to someone with very little body language. So try to adopt a complementary stance, posture and gesticulation to make it more likely that rapport will be created.

Case study: Focus on what is happening not what you think is happening

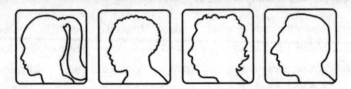

Sheila is a bright and well-educated manager in an international charity, but she was having trouble being taken seriously by some other members of the executive team. All the other team members were men, and that could have been a reason for their dismissive behaviour, but that is not the problem. Sheila had been using this as a reason for her lack of confidence, but it made her feel even less confident.

We taught her how to match the body language and values of the team, and to use questions to clarify the logic of their arguments. We also helped her to tidy up her language so she could be more consultative and less direct when she put forward her ideas. At the next meeting with the executive team she created a 'bring it on' state for herself, and she matched the others all the way through. At the end of the meeting she felt good about her contribution, and confident about the way she interacted with the team. As a result of this, she realised that her previous belief (about her not being taken seriously because she was a woman), whether or not it was true, had been holding her back.

"When you have decided there is a reason for something not working for you, you have formed a belief.

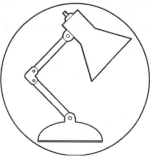

This belief is now part of the problem ... it is of your own making.

A problem can only exist in your mind. Outside your mind there are only circumstances.

When you apply yourself to circumstances and believe that you can succeed you are giving yourself the foundations to succeed at anything."

Exercise: To match your friend's thoughts

Is it really possible to think the same thoughts as another person? Try this exercise with a friend and see.

1 Ask a friend to think of a recent experience and keep it at the front of their mind by picturing the events that happened.

2 As they are doing this match their body posture and breathing as precisely as you can.

3 Put your eyes into the same location, have your hands, arms, legs and feet in exactly the same position, and position your head with the same front/back and left/right tilt.

4 Match the tension in their forehead, jaw, shoulders and hands.

5 When you are as precisely matched as possible notice how you are feeling and describe it to the person you are matching.

6 Guess the mood they are in, and what the experience might be that they are thinking about. You will be surprised how close you can get to what they are actually thinking about.

Can confidence rub off?

Now take this process to match someone you may not know so well but whom you consider to be confident. As you take on their visible persona by matching their body language you will begin to feel as they do inside. If they truly are a confident person then you too will begin to feel the same way.

"Remember that confidence is an illusion, a bit like pulling a rabbit out of a hat: the rabbit does come out of the hat, but there is a magic trick that you did not see that put it in there. By matching someone else's confidence you can appear confident, but no one will notice the techniques you are using to create the perception."

Exercise: Walking the walk

The way you walk can also affect your feeling of confidence. Here is another exercise you can try out in any busy shopping centre.

1 Look for someone who appears confident and follow about three metres behind.

2 Notice how they walk and match it. Match the stride, the weight distribution, the body posture and speed, and notice how you feel inside.

3 Match a few other people and compare the feelings.

4 What kind of attitude goes with the walk? If you are sensitive enough to match accurately you will be able to sense an attitude of mind taking hold.

Keep connecting

Copying, mimicking, imitating different types of the following:

- body language
- posture
- gestures
- voice characteristics

will not only help you to grow more confident, but will also give you more flexibility in your behaviour.

This flexibility will allow you to create connections with more people, build trust with them, seek their help and make more friends. This will help you to feel much more confident about interacting with other people and, remember, it all starts with asking questions.

NLP TRIGGER

RESISTANCE IS A SIGN OF A LACK OF RAPPORT

■ When someone resists an attempt to connect with them it is easy to blame the other person because they are ignorant, foolish, or whatever.

■ When we accept responsibility for the response we realise that we probably did not have enough rapport, and we can fix this.

■ The degree of influence you have with any person will be subject to the amount of rapport you have with them.

Create empowering feelings

"The walls we build around us to keep sadness out also keep out the joy."

Jim Rohn, business philosopher

What you have discovered so far

- To build confidence you need to be 'out there' on the field engaging with others. Otherwise you end up being a mere passive observer. This is why you have emotions – so that you can feel the connection with other people.

- The more you engage the more memorable you become, and the more you will get from your interactions with others. The more you disengage, the smaller you become in the eyes of others.

What you are going to discover

- How 'orange circle' or 'this' thinking can engage and empower us against the negative and disengaged 'blue square' or 'that' associations.

- How 'anchors' tug at your positive and negative outlook and raise or lower your confidence level.

- How to 'anchor' confident 'states' using body language and posture.

- To begin to reprogramme your thinking – and change your physical and emotional responses to situations.

Separating 'this' from 'that'

In our experience and through our NLP programmes we noticed attendees on our confidence courses rely invariably on two simple words to differentiate between projects, tasks and people that they felt fully engaged with, or closely associated with – and those they did not.

1 **This**: quite simply someone describing a project with which they are engaged and associated, is referred to as 'this' project.

2 **That**: conversely, other people's projects with which they are not so engaged or associated are described as 'that' project.

Actually describing things in terms of 'this' and 'that' when time or distance is involved makes absolute sense. For example, you would not refer to a project you completed last year as 'this project'. It does not make sense.

What we discovered was that people referring to 'that project' when it is happening here and now meant that there was something stopping them from becoming fully associated and engaged. Why a person should choose to disengage and distance themselves from anything has many answers, but in many cases we have found the reason to be a lack of confidence.

'Orange circle' versus 'blue square' thinking

We took the 'this' and 'that' proposition, developed it and began to use it to differentiate between useful and unuseful thinking and behaviour.

We decided to make the exercises we developed around the 'this and that' concept even more memorable so we gave them shape and colour.

■ **That** became a blue square – blue representing structure and rules, and a square because you can get stuck in the corners.

■ **This** became an orange circle – orange the colour of energy, growth and flow and a circle because there is nowhere to get stuck.

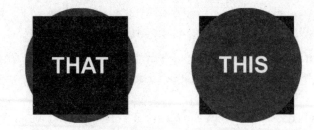

Now here is the interesting bit. You may have seen the symbol for yin and yang, the ancient Chinese symbol for the flow and balance of opposites.

The small dots in the opposite sectors tell us that you cannot have yin without yang, and you cannot have yang without yin. You cannot have hot without cold, wet without dry, light without dark and 'that' without 'this'.

So, symbolically, whenever you find yourself thinking in 'blue squares', that is, lacking in confidence, then the yin-yang principle tells us that there is always a possibility of thinking in 'orange circles'.

"All you have to do is remove the barriers and allow the orange, the true confident you, to shine through."

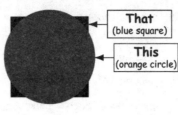

Traditional yin-yang symbol   Blue square – orange circle
version of the yin-yang symbol

- **Yin and yang are opposites.** Everything has its opposite. No one thing is completely yin or completely yang. Each contains the seed of its opposite. For example, winter can turn into summer; 'What goes up must come down.'

- **Yin and yang are interdependent.** One cannot exist without the other. For example, a day cannot exist without night. Light cannot exist without darkness.

Exercise: To 'collapse the connection' with feelings of lack of confidence

- Those barriers to confidence – our thoughts and negative feelings – can be removed. We call this 'collapsing the association or connection'.

- You can use this exercise to free yourself of any negative feelings you have connected to either a person, or an event.

- This exercise uses the concept of yin-yang, which reminds us that, no matter how low your confidence might be, you always have the potential to regain your confidence and all you have to do is focus on it.

- You will now practise:

  (i) how to 'collapse an association' with a feeling of low confidence

(ii) how to replace it with a more empowering feeling by transferring a confident feeling from one context to another.

■ You will need:

(i) some floor space for this exercise; ideally about 3 metres of clear space

(ii) to choose a time that will be uninterrupted for about 15 minutes

(iii) to read through the exercise first so you can complete it without having to refer to the instructions

(iv) to start again from the beginning if you are distracted part way through, or have to stop to follow the instructions

(v) to stay focused throughout the exercise.

A simple 10-step exercise

1 Take a sheet of blank A4 paper and cut out a circle and square as shown by the template provided. Colour the circle with an orange marker pen and the square with a blue marker pen.

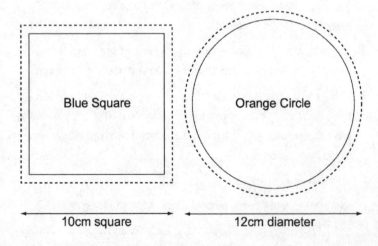

Blue Square

Orange Circle

10cm square

12cm diameter

2 Place the blue square on the floor and stand just behind it.

3 Recall a real situation when you felt you lacked confidence. Remember how unpleasant it felt as you visualise a picture of yourself in that situation. Notice any feelings and in which direction they are moving.

4 Project your feelings down and on to the blue square and then step a metre away to the right. Ask yourself how you would like to feel the next time you are facing this situation. (For example, presumably you would like to have more confidence, maybe some focus and patience, personal power, or some other resource you think will be useful next time.)

5 Now think back to a time when you had these particular resources – you were feeling confident and had all the resources you needed to deal with the situation you were engaged with at the time. Take a few minutes to recall a really good experience where you were feeling very confident. The strength of your feeling in this situation will be used to 'collapse the feeling of low confidence' you have been experiencing.

6 Place the orange circle on the floor at least 3 metres to the right of the blue square and, with your eyes looking upwards, recall the positive situation. Create a bright and colourful picture of yourself.

Make the picture big, turn up the volume of any sounds you can hear, make them sharp and clear. Notice any feelings you have, and make them stronger. Now, if you have not already done so, bring the picture towards you, so close that you become part of it (associated).

7 Notice how your posture has changed. Enjoy this moment and feel good about it. Intensify the feeling by imagining sending it around your body – all the way to your fingertips and toes, and upwards to fill your chest – making you smile in a confident way.

8 When your feelings are strong turn your head and look back to the blue square. Notice how your feelings towards the blue square situation have changed. You have now permanently collapsed the bad feelings.

9 Maintain this positive state, pick up your orange circle and walk back to the blue square.

10 Place the orange circle over the square and imagine yourself dealing with that old situation with this new confident state.

To laugh at one's self

What you have just done is to 'collapse' all the old feelings you had regarding lack of confidence in a specific situation, using resources that you already had in a different scenario. Our research reveals that at the moment of looking back to the 'blue square', people tend to laugh at themselves for having behaved in such a way in the past. This is one of the powerful aspects of the exercise. When we can laugh at ourselves the situation loses its negative charge towards us.

"You have all the resources you need to achieve what you want."

Think 'orange circles'

One of the fundamental beliefs on which NLP is based is that 'you have all the resources you need to achieve what you want'. This exercise demonstrates this clearly. How often have you ever taken internal resources such as confidence, patience, focus, courage, empathy and so on from one scenario to another in this way? Possibly never. Well now you can do it whenever you want to – all you need is your blue square and orange circle.

This technique to rid oneself of negative illusions can help in all sorts of scenarios:

- transfer the confidence perhaps felt with colleagues to social settings where there is a lack of confidence to walk into a room full of strangers
- collapse a fear of taking exams
- collapse a fear of presenting ideas to the Board of Directors
- deal with a colleague who is proving particularly difficult
- stand up to a domineering partner.

The resources are there, they just need to be transferred from one scenario to another. The possibility to succeed is always there, but the way of thinking about it has kept the window of possibility obscured. The orange circle thinking technique can help you to focus more of your natural resources on the possibility of succeeding.

Anchoring confident states

In your unconscious mind you have deeply embedded, or anchored, negative and positive responses to experiences and stimuli. An anchor is a quick connection between an experience or stimulus and a response.

Example 1: A positive anchor

An anchor could be a past romantic moment whilst a particular song was playing; now, whenever you hear the song again, the memories will return bringing with them the same physical and emotional sensations, in this case probably a smile.

Example 2: A negative anchor

Similarly, if you had a bad experience, for example you were involved in a rail accident, now every time you hear the sound of a train – another anchor – you will recall the incident and your body language and emotions will reflect this (you may tense up and screw your face up as the fear returns).

In both of these cases the incident has passed probably never to return in exactly the same way, but you can still tug on the anchored state to evoke exactly the same feelings and physical sensations in response to a trigger.

What are your anchors?

Anchors are all around you, all the time and, depending on whether they are negatively or positively charged, they will have a direct implication for your confidence levels. We are all anchored into stimuli like music or visuals.

Over the next few days see just how many anchors you can identify in the home, travelling to work, in your place of work, travelling home and in your social life. Be consciously aware of what you are thinking. If you find yourself thinking negatively can you track it back to an anchor? For example, have you anchored a response to any of the following:

- your manager's voice, a request to attend a meeting
- a particular voice tone in your partner
- some pictures on an advertising billboard
- a song on the radio?

Ask yourself, 'Is it a useful response?' If yes, leave it alone, if no, then use the 'orange circle' thinking technique to collapse the anchor.

Visualise a yacht anchored in a sunny Caribbean bay, waves lapping on a sandy shore. Now imagine a huge storm cloud obscuring the sun and bringing a descending gloom and breeze and the first spots of rain. Which is your anchor? How often is your boat anchored in the gloom and how often is it anchored in the sunshine?

How to create 'state changes'

You can use the concept of anchors to create 'great states' for yourself once you have taken the decision to step out of your comfort zone to try something new. In NLP we call this a 'state change'. What do we mean by this? Well, it is more than a 'state of mind' or 'the state I'm in' because it includes body language and posture too. Think back to the previous exercise: you collapsed an old anchored response that was no longer useful. Then you created a new response based on resources you already have, which in turn changed your physical and emotional responses. That is a 'state change'.

What you need to do next is to choose an appropriate state for your new challenge and anchor it so that you can resume it any time you want to. For example, to achieve a parachute jump you may wish to acquire a state of calm and focus (a state that you will probably find useful in hundreds of other scenarios as well). Whatever you want to do, it is a good idea to prepare your state of mind-body first. Positive emotions enhance the use of skills whilst negative emotions have the opposite effect: they grip you, and the first thing you lose is the ability to use your skills.

Exercise: To create a positive physical 'anchor'

In the following exercise you are going to create a physical anchor – a trigger – for your state.

■ You are going to choose a small physical action such as squeezing your forefinger and thumb together or pinching your left ear, or similar physical 'trigger'.

■ Make sure it is something:

you can be very precise about

that other people will not notice you doing, and

that you will not trigger accidentally.

For example, if you have a habit of clenching your hands together, this is not a good choice for an anchor as you may trigger your new state at an inappropriate moment.

1 Choose a place where you can feel comfortable and will not be disturbed for about 15 minutes.

2 You can either stand or sit for this exercise. This will depend on the type of state you are going to create for yourself – for example, you may feel that to create a relaxed state you want to be sitting or for an energetic state you may choose to stand.

3 Think of a situation when you were in your chosen state, for example, calm, focused and confident.

4 Choose a 'confidence' anchor such as squeezing your thumb or putting your thumb and finger together.

5 Either recall a situation when you were in this state or create a picture of what it would be like if you were in this situation. Make your picture big and bright, turn up the volume and intensify the feelings.

6 Associate with the picture and, when your feelings rise to their most intense, set your anchor (squeezed fingers or whatever you have chosen to do). Hold this until the feelings begin to fade and then release your anchor.

7 Test your confidence anchor by breaking your state (get up and walk about, talk or think about something else – in NLP we call this breaking state) and then fire it by squeezing your finger and thumb or whatever you have chosen as your anchor. The state of confidence that you have set for yourself will return immediately.

8 Repeat this sequence three to four times to help make it fully automatic.

By using this and the other exercises in this chapter, you have begun to reprogramme your thinking – and change your physical and emotional responses to situations and therefore your behaviour and your results.

If you continue to use these NLP techniques in any situation where you lack confidence you will be surprised at how quickly your confidence will build.

When negative anchors become phobias

Sometimes negative anchored responses can get out of hand. They become phobias. They become what we call 'irrational' responses to normal things such as spiders or insects/creatures of any kind, flying, going over bridges, travelling in lifts or by underground train, being in large places such as supermarkets, a field or in a large crowd, going to the dentist. Such responses can have a huge impact on confidence levels.

Often people with 'phobic' responses, as these are known, will try to hide them because they feel ridiculous or inadequate in some way. They know it is irrational, but do not know how to stop the fear. They watch other people going to the dentist, flying in aeroplanes, travelling in lifts and the underground and ask themselves, 'Why can't I do that?'

If your confidence has been severely affected by a phobic response, take heart, because you can rid yourself of a phobia using the next very straightforward exercise. There is nothing complicated or distressing about it, and there is no need to go through traumatic states to make these changes (as some television programmes would have you believe).

Exercise: To overcome phobias

In this exercise you are going to change an irrational response to an anchor. This is normally conducted with the help of an experienced and competent NLP practitioner but you can certainly give it a solo effort. If you do, make sure you read the instructions carefully and learn the process thoroughly before you begin, to ensure maximum effect.

1 Find a quiet spot where you can sit comfortably in an armchair with both feet firmly on the ground and where you will not be disturbed for at least 20 to 30 minutes.

2 As you sit in the chair imagine you are in a cinema and there is a large white cinema screen up in front of you. On the screen is a black and white still picture of you just before you had your last phobic response.

3 From this position in the chair imagine yourself floating up to the projectionist box from where you can see yourself in the cinema watching the black and white picture of yourself on the screen.

It is comfortable, warm and safe in there.

4 Begin to turn the still picture into a movie, keeping it in black and white, and run it very slowly to the point just after you have had your phobic experience.

5 Freeze-frame the shot – now jump into the picture and run it backwards in full colour to the point where you first started. Everything is in colour, people and things are moving backwards, speech sounds like gobbledygook, and so on.

6 Break state and think about the thing that used to create a phobic response for you. You will find that you will not be able to access the intensity of state you were able to access before the exercise.

Practise this exercise and you will not feel embarrassed or allow phobias to affect your confidence. To help you along the way, here are just two of people overcoming extreme responses.

Case study: Overcoming phobias

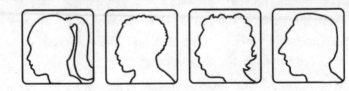

Tim

Tim was a delegate on one of our NLP programmes. It was a beautiful sunny day and one of the other delegates requested that the curtain be drawn across, as the sun was shining directly into her face. As the curtain moved a huge spider ran across the floor. Tim literally flew out of the room and would return only once he was assured the spider had been removed. When he did return he was agitated and felt very embarrassed.

He confessed that spiders affected him so badly that, if he found one at home, he would have to call his partner to remove it.

We took Tim through the exercise to overcome phobias, which took no more than 15 minutes, after which he said spontaneously that he wanted to go and find a spider. Two members of the group searched with him and they managed to locate a spider in the conservatory of the conference centre. Tim was delighted that he was able to watch it crawl about without the phobic reaction. This seemingly small event had a huge impact on his life generally and particularly his confidence levels. Instead of a worried frown he can show a big grin when confronted with his phobia.

Claire

Claire worked for a motoring organisation. Although her role didn't directly involve travelling on the roads, she felt rather silly because she had a fear of bridges. She would take very elongated routes to her destination just to avoid going over a bridge. We took her through the same exercise as for Tim and now she can travel happily anywhere she wants to without having to pre-plan her route to avoid bridges.

During the course of our work we have dealt with all sorts of phobias including responses to the smell of oranges and bananas and even wet hair in the plughole of the shower. They are very real to the person confronting them. Clearing such responses has an enormous effect on confidence as people can now regard themselves as normal and therefore capable of achieving much more.

It is not just the limitations caused by the phobias that are lifted – whole new levels of self-esteem are acquired, lifting the lid on all sorts of potential. Imagine how focused Tim can be now that he is no longer distracted, whatever he is doing, by the fact that a spider may or may not appear at any moment.

NLP TRIGGER

YOUR BEHAVIOUR IS NOT WHO YOU ARE

- You are much more than your behaviour.

- You have hidden potential just like everyone else.

- Personal change is a common occurrence for people who make the decision to change. If you look around you will find plenty of examples of people who have learned new skills, changed their beliefs and values, and who are demonstrating new capabilities.

- Some people remain stuck because they either do not want to change, or do not know how to change. There is no excuse for either of these predicaments – some people just prefer to suffer and dwell in a sea of self-directed sympathy.

- That you are reading this book is an indication that you are loosening the chains of self-doubt already and becoming ever more engaged with life.

Step outside your comfort zone

"If you hear a voice within you say 'you cannot paint,'
then by all means paint, and that voice will be silenced."
Vincent Van Gogh, Impressionist painter

What you have discovered so far

- Building self-confidence is no different from learning anything else.

- By doing the exercises you will feel your confidence grow.

- You learn one step at a time and, the more you practise, the more self-confident you will become.

What we are going to discover

- You are going to realise the importance of using your mind in a slightly different way in order to grow your confidence.

- You are going to use your imagination to take control of your emotional state, and this will set you free to do the things that deep down you know you want to do.

- Each time you use one of the NLP techniques in this book to gain confidence, you are exercising your mind and opening it up to new possibilities.

- You can take the ideas and exercises in this chapter to form part of your daily, if not hourly, practice.

- So shed your skin of low confidence and grow a new one, which is bigger, brighter and more aspirational than ever before.

"It is amazing how quickly your mind is able to grasp new ideas when you stop judging, and become increasingly curious to learn. Remember, the mind is like a parachute – it works best when it is open."

Self control – the 'mindful' over the 'mindless'

You have not just one amazingly alert and receptive mind: you have the potential for two, or more, minds. In fact people often say, 'I'm in two minds' to declare they are undecided, for example. Well, one way of thinking about becoming more confident is to imagine you have two minds, **but** where one is used to control the other. This is where self-control begins – in the relationship between your two minds.

Some people seem to have lots of self-control and are able to resist temptations and distractions. Others can be seen losing the battle and giving in to all kinds of indulgences and distractions, which result in bad feelings and low self-esteem.

Your unconscious, habitual mind

- The mind that needs to be controlled is the one that stores all your habits and automatic responses.

- This mind is usually referred to as your unconscious mind because it is able to operate without you being aware of it.

- It is responsible for all your automatic behaviour and routine actions, including the way you communicate with commonly used phrases and sequences of dialogue.

- It is also responsible for all the thinking and behaviour associated with low confidence and feelings of anxiety, fear and anger.

- Controlling your unconscious mind is the way to increase your confidence.

"What you capture in your mind to be able to remember experiences is only your perception of events at the time they occurred."

Eternal sunshine of the spotless mind

Your unconscious mind can be very easily confused: for example how do you **know** the difference between something you have seen and something you have imagined?

What you capture in your mind to be able to remember experiences is only your perception of events at the time they occurred. But perceptions are mainly illusionary – formed through our individual make-up of values and beliefs.

Of course you will remember events, but the meaning you put on those events is uniquely yours and anyone's guess. Moreover, it is fluid so, as you learn and grow, your perceptions and meanings change with you.

Simply grasping that the mind works in this way offers a great advantage to becoming more confident. So you can use your higher, conscious mind to give new directions to the unconscious mind that imagines, remembers and constructs your inner illusionary experience.

Exercise: Do you sense danger or see opportunities?

When you react to events you have two basic choices:

1 You can react as if the event is something that will **nourish** you; you see a certain experience as an opportunity.

2 You can react as if it will **harm** you; you see the same experience as a threat. If you lack confidence then the variety of events which cause this fundamental reaction to kick in is far greater.

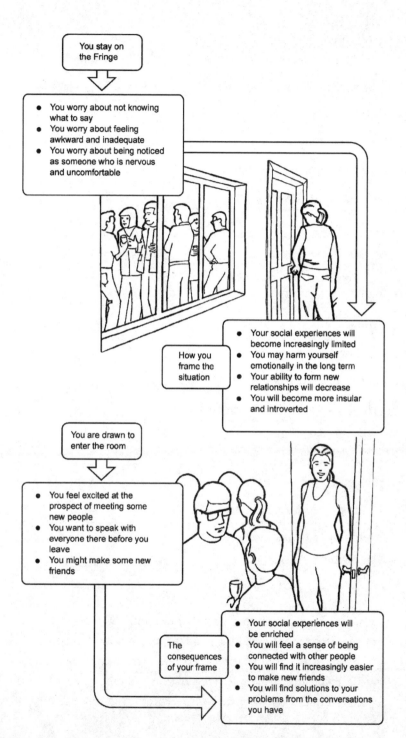

You stay on the Fringe

- You worry about not knowing what to say
- You worry about feeling awkward and inadequate
- You worry about being noticed as someone who is nervous and uncomfortable

How you frame the situation

- Your social experiences will become increasingly limited
- You may harm yourself emotionally in the long term
- Your ability to form new relationships will decrease
- You will become more insular and introverted

You are drawn to enter the room

- You feel excited at the prospect of meeting some new people
- You want to speak with everyone there before you leave
- You might make some new friends

The consequences of your frame

- Your social experiences will be enriched
- You will feel a sense of being connected with other people
- You will find it increasingly easier to make new friends
- You will find solutions to your problems from the conversations you have

Tick the relevant box for each activity:	Your immediate reaction	
Activity	**Nourishing**	**Limiting**
Meeting someone new		
Being at a party		
Complaining about poor service		
Asking for your money back		
Taking a test or exam		
Going on a first date		
Challenging a superior at work		
Telling someone how you feel about them		
Applying for a new job or project		
Attending a job interview		
Flying in a commercial passenger jet		
Giving a presentation to a group		
Saying, 'No,' to a colleague or senior manager		
Starting a new business venture		
Telling a joke or funny story at a company event		

While it is reasonable to expect that to jump out of an aeroplane for the first time might kick in fear reaction for some people, it is less reasonable to expect the same reaction just by walking into a room full of people. Nevertheless, there are many who react as if in danger when faced with entering a room full of new people.

The doorways of perception

Gaining confidence is all about tipping the balance away from perceptions of threat towards sensing that opportunities are possible. As your self-confidence increases, so the varieties of experience that cause you to feel in danger reduce. Instead of seeing the danger in experiences, you begin to see opportunities and benefits.

- This does not mean that you say, 'Yes' to every dangerous proposition that comes your way, and become reckless; rather you are able to have more choice about being involved in more pursuits that nourish you as a person.

- This is not just about being optimistic and positive with everything and everybody; rather your new-found confidence allows you to experience, without fear or anxiety, so many more aspects of life.

- You may still choose to say, 'No' to certain things, but your choices are made for practical purposes rather than for reducing your fear.

"The state of health of your thinking determines how you behave."

Everything begins with a thought

Just how many different experiences cause you to feel in danger when there is no real physical threat? And how do you address every one of them so that confidence is built regardless of the experience?

Think through these statements:

■ Every response you have begins with one single thought.

■ This one thought attracts others of a similar nature until you have a cluster of similar thoughts occupying your mind.

■ When you adopt a certain emotional state it tends to infect whatever thoughts are in your mind – so even the most innocent of thoughts can become laced with fear, anxiety, depression, anger or even indifference.

■ When thoughts and emotions mix, it is the emotion that usually dictates the outcome. It is the emotion that conjures up lame excuses:

> for not doing things
>
> for making you ill when there is really no external cause
>
> for covering up a lack of will power
>
> for putting blame somewhere so you can be relieved of the responsibility for not pursuing what you really want.

So the state of health of your thinking determines how you behave: if you are unhappy about the way you feel then you definitely need to build confidence to collapse this unhappiness. For example, even if you think you would like to meet someone you are attracted to, by the time you have absorbed the thought of making an introduction, your emotional state, say of fear of engagement, means your behaviour is working against you.

"Your mind is unable to process a negative instruction. Holding in your mind the notion of 'being on time' is more likely to get you there on time than the notion of 'not being late'."

Know what you want

The famous martial arts teacher, movie star and philosopher Bruce Lee advised anyone with a desire to 'keep your mind on what you want and off what you don't want'. This is very practical advice.

You need to know what you want first:

- Do you know what it feels like to really want something?
- So much so that you will allow nothing to get in your way?

It could be a relationship, or a business idea you want to launch, or a career ambition. A self-confident person would have a very strong sense of being driven (by their own higher mind) towards achieving what they want.

Hold a positive thought

You tend to get what you hold in your thoughts – so no matter how much you try and not think of a red elephant, you have to think of it. This is why you will get better results telling yourself that you will 'be on time' as opposed to 'not to be late'.

Your mind is unable to process a negative instruction: so holding in your mind the notion of 'being on time' is more likely to get you there on time than the notion of 'not being late'. A confident person is much more likely to be holding positive images in their mind of what they want, rather than what they do not want.

"People who fear the worst usually end up getting it."

Talking yourself 'down'

A low-confidence person, on the other hand, tends to surround their desire with thoughts of difficulty and possible ways to fail:

this in turn dissipates the energy and drive, and raises all sorts of questions about their ability to succeed. People who fear the worst usually end up getting it.

A common feature in the thinking of someone who lacks confidence is frequent negative internal dialogue, or self-talk. Having a head full of tape loops that keep repeating, telling you:

- how incompetent you are compared with other people
- how badly things might work out or
- how no one is listening to you or interested in you

is bound to knock your confidence and keep you feeling low.

These negative loops keep spinning when you focus your attention in on yourself. The consequence of this is that you have to stop listening to what people are saying, and this makes you feel even worse when you realise you have lost the plot somewhere down the line.

Accentuate the positive

Think about the Van Gogh quote at the start of this chapter: you are going to create confident self-talk by deciding what you want, and then stop thinking about 'you'. Keep your mind focused on what you are going to do and try this exercise.

Exercise: To create a positive inner voice and tone

Listen to your inner voice and notice what kind of voice it is.

- Is it your own voice or someone else's?
- What kind of tone, speed and volume does the voice have?
- If it were more of a confident voice how would it sound?

■ What words would you give it?

Try some of these words and feel how they fit for you:

C'mon, let's go!
Right. Time to let go of all this and make a positive move!
OK, let's get on with it!
Enough thinking - it's time for action!
Bring it on!
This is going to be so cool!
Go for it!

By all means try out some of your own phrases, just make sure that
when you say them you feel more motivated to get up and do
something you might not have done before.

Exercise: Fine-tuning your posture to match your tone

1 If you have lots of inner dialogue you will find that your head
   will be angled down and your eyes looking down. This is the
   position a person takes when indulging in self-talk in this way.
   You only have to watch people walking down a busy high
   street to notice how many people are doing this.

2 So the very simplest thing you can do to turn off your dialogue
   is to lift your head up and focus your vision somewhere above
   the horizon line.

3 Check your posture also and make sure you are holding
   yourself up straight and not humped or slouched. It is much

more difficult to keep your self-talk going when you are holding yourself in this way.

4 Just notice more about your surroundings and keep your attention focused out on the environment.

This very simple change will be enormously beneficial.

Decide what you want, and talk yourself 'up'

If you were to 'shadow' a highly confident person and a person who lacks confidence, you would notice some clear differences in the language they use. The following comparison is a typical example of what you might hear.

Talking 'down': lacking self-confidence	Talking 'up': high self-confidence
I might not like …	I will give it a go and see what
Be reasonable …	happens.
That is unrealistic …	Come on, what the heck, give it a
It would not work …	go!
I could not do …	Sounds like a real challenge!
It is just not me …	OK, let me see what happens.
We will never find it …	I have not tried it yet.
It will be too busy …	I will give it my best shot.
They probably will not have one …	It has to be somewhere.
Do you think I should …	It will be busy but what the heck.
What if it does not work?	I wonder if they will have one.
It is bound to go wrong.	I have decided to …

I will do it when everything is right.	Let us find out if it works.
	It will either work or it will not.
I would like to, but …	Let us get moving soon as we can.
I am comfortable when …	Yes, I would like to try that.
	Bring it on.

Telling the confident from the unconfident

"The danger with keeping past failings in the present is that you generally stop looking for ways to improve."

Do not let the past rule the present

There is a common tendency in the use of language to keep past experiences current by explaining them in the present tense. For example, you might hear someone say, 'I'm no good at doing accounts/DIY/language/dancing' [and so on].

Unless the person is doing it now, it is untrue. Maybe in the past, perhaps only yesterday, they tried to calculate something or drill a hole in the wall and found it difficult. So a truer statement would be: 'I found it difficult to calculate my tax yesterday'.

This second statement recognises that the experience was in the past and opens up the possibility that, if this person really would like to improve, they can find a way to learn. The danger with keeping past failings in the present is that you generally stop looking for ways to improve.

Stop orienting the mind towards the negative

Letting your mind dwell on how a scenario might unfold and what the result will be is common but dangerous. This is **not** the same positive visualisation. In fact it is the opposite. If the mind is oriented towards the negative then the result is usually negative also. The conclusion then is to avoid the scenario because you have already decided it will end unpleasantly. You expect things to turn out for the worse and so they probably do. Just how many experiences are being blocked in this way?

Think 'possible' over 'impossible'

What you consider 'possible' and 'impossible' again is just an illusion of the mind. The more pursuits you label as 'impossible', the blander your life becomes. To really gauge our capacity for what is 'possible' consider famous and not-so-famous people who have excelled against overwhelming odds. For example, think of Nelson Mandela and do you wonder what he had to do to achieve what he did for his country? He overcame despair and hatred with hope and dignity and his autobiography *Long Walk to Freedom* is a must read for anyone seeking to stretch their horizons of possibility. The following case studies make the point sharply.

Case study: Dr William Tan – focusing on abilities, not disabilities

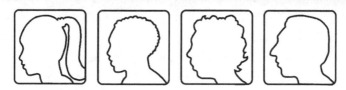

We were privileged to share a platform with this highly inspirational Singaporean who has accomplished so much in the areas of sport and medicine. Dr Tan greets life's unfortunate setbacks and challenges with grace and vibrancy. His perseverance is legendary: he has overcome obstacles, especially when people told him he could not do something due to his disability (he was paralysed from the waist down by polio at the age of three). He considers the word 'cannot' as the most disgusting swear word in our language. He chooses to focus on his abilities and not disabilities. He sets high standards for himself, in his life as an athlete (he has a set a target of 10 marathons across 7 continents in 65 days), as an educator, as a professional healer and researcher, and as a person who believes in making a difference in the lives of others.[1]

Case study: Tomorr Kokona

Tomorr is the founder of the Culture and Arts Dance Challenge. They coach over 500 young people across London each week and put on a

[1] Go to www.willpower.com.sg to learn more about this exceptional individual.

yearly dance competition at Wembley Arena. This year 800 children from 60 London schools took part in the event.

Tomorr arrived in the UK from Albania in 1991 via Spain where he spent three years working with the Spanish National Theatre and Classical Ballet of Madrid. In Albania he trained with the Albanian National Ballet School. When he first arrived he had lots of ideas about what he wanted to do to help children at risk of offending to lead a better life than he had under the Albanian form of communism. We were privileged to work with Tomorr on one of our programmes whilst he was formulating his ideas and developing the confidence to get his latest project off the ground.

Case study: Sue – the confidence to let go of self-indulgence

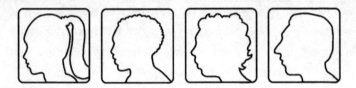

In order to have low self-esteem a person has to be constantly looking inwards, worrying about themselves and how they appear to others. This can also be described as high self-indulgence. Sue arrived on our NLP programme with exactly this level of self-esteem. Her job as a market researcher for a mobile phone company was not going as she would have liked, her relationship had broken up some time before, and her confidence was at an all-time low. She had stopped paying attention to her appearance because she felt it was a waste of time and when she went out she spent her time gathering evidence to prove to herself that she was right to have low self-esteem.

Taking on board our NLP techniques, Sue became aware of her thinking patterns and the mayhem she was causing for herself inside her head – and she was able to reprogramme her thinking. She had the confidence to go out and meet new people from which a new relationship developed. She switched jobs after being approached by the market research company she had previously hired who appreciated her marketing skills and mobile phone experience.

Stop thinking it has to be perfect first

Sometimes you may feel you want to achieve something, but prevent yourself from doing so through making excuses. This can often manifest itself in the requirement to have everything perfect before you begin. When you can realise that perfection is just an illusion, and another excuse for inertia, you will be able to overcome this habit and get stuck in! Whilst you will want to plan, the more you wait for some illusionary state of perfection, the more you will ponder and sit and think and ... do nothing. There is nothing stopping you but yourself.

A well-known tenet in Hindu Vedic philosophy states that everything already is perfect, as it was meant to be. So rather than wait for a moment of perfection, understand how things work, observe relationships, notice reactions, and you will learn to work with them. Grasp hold of this idea and cling to it.

Confidence is tested only in unfamiliar territory

Do you now feel more inspired to step outside your comfort zone and do something uncharacteristic? Remember, confidence is tested only in unfamiliar territory. For example, you may think someone is confident at business: you look at them and say, 'Ah, they're confident,' but what you are really doing is trying to interpret the way you are responding to them when you see them, look at their body language, and hear them talk. We have used the 'confidence label' to generalise and make them 'a confident person', when in fact they are simply 'good at business' and know what they are doing. See them in another scenario, driving a car for instance, and they may be all over the place.

'You're fired!'

Think of the bullish business boys and girls in the TV reality show *The Apprentice*. They might appear confident in one role but when Sir Alan Sugar deliberately puts them into unfamiliar territory and roles, sometimes out of their comfort zones, their confidence is shot to pieces. And while they are often 'bringing it on' in their 'house' they become quite cowered and pleading in the boardroom.

NLP TRIGGER

IF IT IS POSSIBLE FOR ONE PERSON THEN IT IS POSSIBLE FOR OTHERS

■ You know that you can do so many things that you see other people doing.

■ Apart from disabilities (and, as we have seen, these do not need to be a barrier to achievement) the only limitation is self-imposed, inside your head.

■ So the possibility for you to do whatever you decide is worthwhile and meaningful is always present.

■ You are the one in control of your **limitations** and **potential**.

Who is knocking your confidence?

"Nobody can make you feel inferior without your consent."

Eleanor Roosevelt, First Lady of the United States 1933–45

What you have discovered so far

- When thoughts and emotions mix, it is the emotion that dictates the outcome. It is the emotion that conjures up lame excuses and predicts negative outcomes.

- A confident person is more likely to be holding positive images in their mind of what they want, rather than what they do not want. 'I'm looking forward to this,' they think rather than, 'I hope it's not going to be boring.'

- What you consider 'possible' and 'impossible' is just an illusion of the mind. The more pursuits you label as 'impossible', the blander your life becomes.

- You need to eradicate negative self-talk and put enthusiasm into your inner voice tone.

- Confidence is tested only in unfamiliar territory **so** step outside your comfort zone and do something uncharacteristic.

What you are going to discover

- People often tell us that they have had their confidence knocked – a statement that suggests that they have been confident at one time but something has happened for this to change.

- How does confidence become knocked and what type of force has such control of our thinking to allow confidence to become knocked?

- A more important question is, perhaps, 'Who is doing the knocking?'

"Life is about choice – we can either choose to have our confidence knocked or we can choose to think differently."

Case study: Tanya – How confidence is knocked

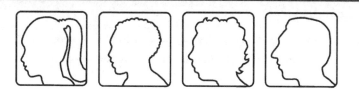

Tanya told us that her confidence had been knocked because, upon returning to work in a call centre operation after maternity leave, Bill, a member of her team, expressed in no uncertain terms that he felt he should have her job as customer services manager. He continued to be unpleasant and obstructive in all that he did in an attempt to unsettle Tanya. The other five members of the team welcomed her back and she was able to continue a healthy and productive working relationship with them. But Tanya could not get Bill out of her mind. She was allowing him to dominate her thoughts and an inordinate amount of her time was being spent focusing on her working relationship with Bill. Her confidence was being knocked.

The balance sheet

Tanya's positives

- She has a strong value around building productive relationships at work.
- She is interested in her team's welfare and takes time and effort to make sure that they are progressing in a way that is good for them and for the organisation.

Tanya's negatives

- Her value had been challenged by Bill and she developed the belief that because she could not build a relationship with Bill she could not be a good manager.

■ Consequently every time they met, her physical and emotional responses changed. Her stress levels would rise and she would become defensive.

■ She expended so much energy trying to rebuild the working relationship with Bill that the rest of the team began to resent the situation.

Reframe the problem

1 We encouraged her to get it in perspective. Bill represented only one sixth of her team – the other five people would be perfectly happy if she gave them as much attention and energy as she gave Bill.

2 We helped her to reframe her belief – one poor relationship does not mean she is a bad manager, it simply means she has some exploring to do.

3 We engaged with her to be curious about the reasons for Bill's unpleasantness. Using the 'orange circle' thinking technique (see page 109) we helped her to collapse the negative feelings she had whenever she was in Bill's company and replace them with the same feelings she had when she was in the company of other members of her team.

4 We suggested she should imagine that Bill represented a blue square. Her challenge now was to find as many positive orange circles in relation to Bill and focus on these whenever she communicated with him. If he chose to be unpleasant then she was to point out to him that such behaviour was his choice.

It worked – it was not long before Tanya had taken back control of her thinking and feelings around Bill; he perceived the new Tanya and began to behave in a very different way towards her.

Life is about choice – we can either choose to have our confidence knocked or we can choose to think differently. In order to think differently it is necessary to suspend judgement long enough to explore other possible meanings for the things that happen. On the next page is a graphic representation of the choice that Tanya had.

Choose to think differently

- Tanya had placed a meaning on Bill's behaviour that had created a negative illusion for her, that is, she must be a bad manager.

- Not only was she storing up negative stuff about Bill, she was also virtually deleting what was going on with the rest of the team (with whom her professional relationship was absolutely fine) and judging her own performance on just one person.

- The human mind is very good at placing meanings on all sorts of things that eventually get translated as, 'I've had my confidence knocked.'

- Tanya's relationship with Bill became much healthier when she started to look for ways to help Bill to achieve what he wanted.

Lightening the load on one's mind

There is an ancient Zen Buddhist story used to illustrate the search for enlightenment that vividly captures Tanya's obsession. Two monks were travelling together on a muddy road with a heavy rain still falling. Coming around a bend they met a lovely young woman in a silk kimono and sash unable to get across the crossroads. 'Come on, young girl,' said Tanzan, the elder of the two monks, at once, as he lifted the lady up in his arms and carried her over the mud, placed her down and continued the journey. Ekido, the younger monk, was silent until later that night when the two monks found lodgings at a temple. Then he could not hold his silence any longer and had to speak. 'Brother,' he said, 'we monks do not go near females, especially not young and lovely ones. It is dangerous. Why did you do that?' 'I left the girl at the crossroads,' replied Tanzan, 'are you still carrying her in your mind?'

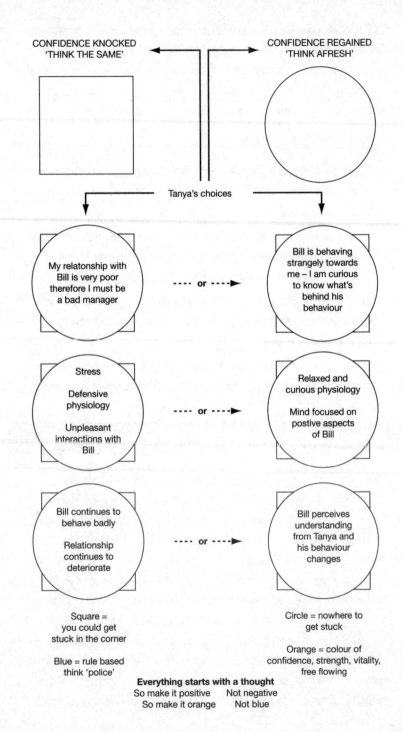

CONFIDENCE KNOCKED
'THINK THE SAME'

CONFIDENCE REGAINED
'THINK AFRESH'

Tanya's choices

My relationship with Bill is very poor therefore I must be a bad manager

---- or ---->

Bill is behaving strangely towards me – I am curious to know what's behind his behaviour

Stress

Defensive physiology

Unpleasant interactions with Bill

---- or ---->

Relaxed and curious physiology

Mind focused on postive aspects of Bill

Bill continues to behave badly

Relationship continues to deteriorate

---- or ---->

Bill perceives understanding from Tanya and his behaviour changes

Square = you could get stuck in the corner

Blue = rule based think 'police'

Circle = nowhere to get stuck

Orange = colour of confidence, strength, vitality, free flowing

Everything starts with a thought
So make it positive   Not negative
So make it orange   Not blue

In a similar way Tanya had been carrying Bill in her head ever since she returned to work. She had been making Bill much larger than life, in her head, and it was time to let him go. Bill could no longer knock her confidence.

Exercise: What experience have you had to knock your confidence?

Here are a few possibilities.

Tick the appropriate box

1 Someone said something to you. ☐

2 Someone encouraged you to go for a promotion that you did not get. ☐

3 Someone commented negatively on your appearance. ☐

4 You had a bad experience giving a presentation. ☐

5 Your boss did not like the way you approached a task or project. ☐

6 You took on a management role that did not go well. ☐

7 You have applied for a number of roles that you have not been offered. ☐

8 You have put on some weight. ☐

9 You have been ill. ☐

10 A long-term relationship has broken up. ☐

11 You had an accident. ☐

12 You were the victim of an attack. ☐

If any of these has happened to you, take some time to be curious about the meaning you have placed on the event. For example:

- What meaning have you attached to putting on weight?
- What meaning have you placed on not being able to get the job you would like?
- Ask yourself, is this really true?
- What alternative meaning could I put on it that would be more empowering for me?

Other NLP ways to reframe negativity

There are a huge variety of NLP techniques you can use – you may find some easier than others – but the following examples are good for starters.

1 Make 'light' of 'heavy' feelings

Case study: Toby – Response to confidence knocked – avoiding confrontation

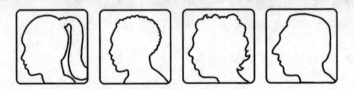

Toby took a job as marketing manager with a new company. The culture was very different from what he had known in his previous company. Because he was a caring person he would go out of his way to avoid inconveniencing anyone, especially other managers. Whilst this did not pose a problem in his last company, it was very different here where he was expected to assert his ideas and suggestions regardless of what other people thought. He did not feel very comfortable about this, especially when others would assert their views with him.

The way he framed his thinking around this experience was to decide that he did not fit in with the way people wanted to get things done.

This decision caused him to lack confidence, pull back and limit his contact with others. His peers judged this behaviour to mean that he was not up to the job, and so a destructive cycle was set in motion.

Through our NLP course we were able **to help Toby reframe his meaning** about their behaviour, and to do so we were a little provocative. It went something like this:

- 'So Toby, you have plenty of marketing experience and therefore have plenty to offer your new company. How come you are choosing to withhold this capability because you are afraid of putting someone's nose out of joint??!'
- 'Isn't this what everyone else is doing anyway?'
- 'Surely you don't expect them to suddenly change overnight and ask you what you think, do you?'
- 'If the only thing that is holding you back is the way you feel, then get a different feeling from somewhere.'
- 'You do have other feelings, don't you?'
- 'Which one can put you in the frame of mind to help you get your experience and ideas over to this argumentative bunch?'
- 'Think back to a time when you had an assertive feeling, and now imagine what you are going to say at the next marketing meeting.'

If the dialogue above seems a little harsh to you, it is, because there is no tone of voice indicated. It was actually delivered in a very humorous way, suggesting to Toby that he had been absurd in holding back his experience. In reality, when we analyse the situations in which we avoid confrontation or take a negative view of something, we are being ridiculous and absurd in some way. When you take a detached view of some of your own negative feelings you too will see the absurdity in the situation.

Conclusion: have a good laugh at yourself

When you can realise your own absurdity in a situation you can begin to laugh at yourself. They say that laughter is the best therapy, and we know this to be so true from our coaching experiences. When a person is so attached to negative perceptions of self, feelings get very 'heavy'. The simplest and quickest way out of this heaviness is to see the absurdity in your situation – make 'light' of it – and have a jolly good laugh at yourself. You will feel an immediate relief.

2 See the absurdity

Case study: David – Response to confidence knocked – freezing on stage

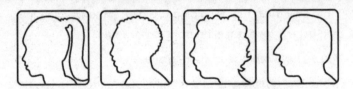

David belongs to a t'ai chi school where he is often called upon to perform 'moving meditations' of this martial art at public events. At a recent performance Lee, a highly skilled student, totally forgot a sequence of movements he had practised many thousands of times. The result was that he froze on the stage while the remainder of his team carried on with their synchronised display.

At the end Lee said that he always gets nervous before a performance and forgets what to do. He was so worried about making a wrong move that he created the problem for himself.

David responded as follows, 'So Lee, when you walk onto the performance area you are worrying about doing something wrong, even though you have practised thousands of times. It seems absurd that such confidence can disappear in the presence of an audience.

'I wonder how easy it would be for you instead to imagine telling the audience how they had better get ready to be amazed at what you are going to do.

'What if you were to laugh at your skill, because it is so easy for you, and think about how amazed the audience will be when they see what you can do. How will this change the way you feel?'

Conclusion

Lee could see the absurdity, and connected with this different feeling at the next performance, which he carried off with near perfection.

3 Kick the stress of expectation into touch

Case study: Clara – Response to confidence knocked – need to seek approval and make better impact

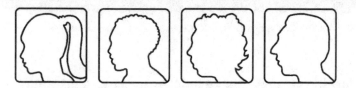

■ Sometimes the stress of having to live up to an expectation, either someone else's, or one that is self-imposed, can cause confidence to wane.

- It is also very tiring to try and be someone you are not, or to succeed at something you have little value for, or lack the appropriate skills.

- It is as though no matter how much effort you put in you get no closer to meeting the expectation.

Clara is small of stature and was having difficulty in getting people to listen to her. For a number of years her appraisals at work had included a reference to her needing to 'make more of an impact'.

Not surprisingly, when she arrived on one of our programmes, her outcomes included, 'I need to make more of an impact on people within my organisation.'

By the middle of the second day, after a series of 'light bulb moments', Clara suddenly declared, 'I don't need this outcome any more – I do my job well and I know how to build rapport with people. I have been putting far too much credence on "making an impact" when actually, if I just be me, I can do it naturally.'

Conclusion

- Supported by a belief imposed on her by other people Clara had been totally focused in her efforts 'to make an impact' rather than on the job-related outcome she was trying to achieve.

- Leaving the programme with a big smile on her face she took a flipchart pen and drew a line through her outcome stating that, 'From now on I'm going to be me.'

How to reframe your responses using visualisation

There are a number of ways to deal with unwanted thinking patterns that lead to lack of confidence.

1 Turn on the camera lens technique

1 Imagine you are looking through the lens of a camcorder at the event that causes you to lose confidence.

2 Zoom right in and fine-tune the colour – make it big and bright.

3 Turn up the volume so that you can hear clearly all the sounds associated with the image.

4 Notice how this strengthens the negative feelings.

5 Now imagine turning the zoom control the other way very fast. As you do so the picture disappears into the distance, the sound disappears and all you can see is a small pin-sized image in the far distance.

6 Compare the feelings you have now with the feelings you had when the zoom control was turned the other way.

You can use your imagination in this way to change your feelings instantly. Once you have learned how to do this you will have increasing control over the way you feel.

2 Hang on to the swish technique

Use this technique to reprogramme your visual imagery and change how you feel about something.

1 Create a picture in your mind of yourself in a real situation in which you felt you lacked confidence.

2 Bring the picture up close.

3 Make it big, clear and bright, and turn up any sounds.

4 Notice the intensity of the feelings you are experiencing.

5 Notice also the location of the feelings and whether or not they are moving in any particular direction.

6 Put a frame around the picture and 'park it' to one side for a moment.

7 Break your state by getting up and moving around or simply thinking about something ordinary.

8 Now create in your mind a picture of how you would like to be in this situation or of another time where you were really feeling confident.

9 Do the same with this picture – bring it up close, make it bright and clear, be aware of the sounds and the intensity of the positive feelings this picture creates.

10 Now start to push the picture away and as it moves further and further away watch the colour drain out of the bottom of the picture.

11 Move it further into the distance and make it smaller and smaller, and turn down the volume so the sounds become hardly audible any more. Keep doing this until your picture resembles a small grey postage stamp in the distance.

12 Break your state as in step 7.

13 Now bring back the original unpleasant picture so that it is just in front of your face and place the small grey postage stamp that is now the positive image in one corner.

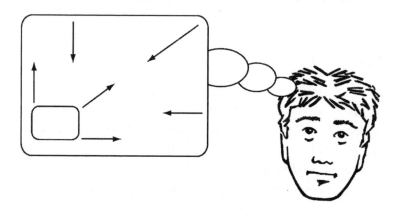

14 On the count of '1–2–3 swish' instantaneously collapse the big picture and make the small picture burst into glorious technicolour replacing the unpleasant picture as you do so (the tonal sounds of the command will help you in this step).

15 Repeat this several times until you find it impossible to bring back the unpleasant picture. Your mind will want to automatically think of the newly programmed images, thus putting you in a much more resourceful state with positive feelings.

3 Reframe illusions and negative thoughts

We have seen already in this chapter that it is very easy to quickly put a meaning on someone else's behaviour and then continue to behave as though it is true. Choosing to put a negative meaning on it has a number of consequences, including making yourself feel bad and placing the responsibility for feeling bad in someone else's hands. From here you create a negative state for the next time you find yourself in such a situation and so the spiral continues to play itself out.

NLP reframing techniques can effectively break this cycle of negativity. Take Chloe's example in the following case study.

Case study: Chloe

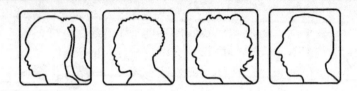

Chloe believed her boss was always trying to catch her out. Whenever she approached him with a query he would challenge her in some way, asking her questions, pointing out things that had not previously occurred to her. She would come away from these interactions feeling very uncomfortable and as though she was never going to be able to please him or come up to the standard he appeared to be demanding.

We helped Chloe to reframe her thinking by asking her: 'What else do you think he could be doing other than "trying to catch you out" when he is asking you these questions?'

After a short while she was able to view the interactions differently, having reframed her thinking into: 'He wants me to succeed and be more confident in my decision making.'

The type of reframing we offered Chloe is called **content reframing** – in other words we offered her an alternative meaning to his behaviour.

We could also have offered her a **context reframe** suggesting that, although she found her boss's questioning technique difficult to deal with at times, it did work well in the context of a team meeting when he is trying to get everyone to think more laterally about a project. In other words, the behaviour has a really positive impact in a different context.

- Reframing your thinking in this way is a powerful technique that requires you to be open minded and to recognise when you are forming a judgement.

- Choosing to place a positive meaning on such behaviour opens up the possibilities of positive outcomes.

- The first step in reframing your thinking is to ask the simple question, 'What else could such behaviour mean?' In Chloe's case, believing that her boss has her interests at heart and is helping her to succeed is much more likely to have a positive impact on the relationship and her ongoing success than thinking he is trying to catch her out.

So what if Chloe's boss really was trying to catch her out?

The first question to ask here would be, 'What would be his purpose in doing so?' The purpose invariably will have a positive intention – this could be either for you or for him personally. Once you can identify this positive intention you can find other ways to help him satisfy it.

Thus you are taking positive action to help someone else and in doing so are gaining in your own confidence and influencing skills which people around you will notice.

Conclusion

1 Judging the behaviour and acting from a defensive position invariably results in tears.

2 Finding the positive intention behind the behaviour opens up the possibility of both parties winning.

3 Reframing your thinking in this way will enable you to focus on the more positive aspects of the things that occur in your experience and this will, in turn, have a positive impact on your level of confidence.

NLP TRIGGER

EVERY BEHAVIOUR HAS
A POSITIVE INTENTION

- Although sometimes this may not appear to be true when we look around at the awful things that happen in the world, if you dig deep enough you will find that every behaviour a person demonstrates has a positive intention behind it.

- The question is 'for whom?'

- Positive intentions are often attempting to satisfy an unmet need such as a sense of personal security, recognition or acceptance.

- Whilst intentions are usually positive, behaviour can have a negative effect.

- The secret to helping people to change their negative behaviour is to get to the root of the positive intention behind it.

- Help them to satisfy the intention with positive rather than negative behaviour.

- People do not generally set out to knock your confidence – this is a state you choose as a result of something happening.

Confident body, confident mind

"Know, then, whatever cheerful and serene supports the mind, supports the body too."
From *The Art of Preserving Health* by John Armstrong, poet (1709–79)

What you have discovered so far

- Life is about choice – you can either choose to have your confidence knocked or you can choose to think differently.

- If you reframe how you think you can change how you feel.

- The more you are able to laugh at your absurdity, the lighter you will feel and the more relaxed you will become.

- If you are trying to meet an expectation that does not fit for you, expect to become stressed. Dropping these expectations and 'lightening your load' is a great way to de-stress.

What you are going to discover

- Confidence, and lack of it, is displayed outwardly in our 'body language'.

- In our experience, the more rigid the body the more rigid the mind (this applies to people whose bodies have become rigid through lack of exercise, rather than physical disability).

- To underplay this would be to deprive you of one of the most effective methods of becoming a confident person.

- Making simple body 'adjustments' can help you think more confidently.

- Sometimes shifting your body language on a very small scale can bring quite significant results.

- This is why meditation can also be very beneficial: it relaxes your body and the mind follows.

"Your mind and body are inextricably connected and act as one entity."

Basic body language

- Every single thought you have transfers into your body somewhere so that, as you grow older, your body takes on the posture that reflects how you have been thinking all your life.

- The more you adopt a certain way of thinking, the more your body will reflect this. If you want evidence just look around at people you know.

- Those with the most flexible and open minds also have flexible and open body language. The reverse is also true.

- People who have fixed minds and are unwilling to open up to new ideas develop fixed, closed body language.

The link from mental tension to physical tension – hypertension

Your mind and body are inextricably connected and act as one entity. This is how you become stressed. Just look at football managers or coaches during a televised match: they are drawn and hunched in their seats and chewing gum if their team is losing, jumping up and down cock-a-hoop and hand clapping if their team scores a goal, and pacing up and down irate with hands gesticulating if the referee's decision goes against them.

Stress starts in your mind and works its way through to your body which is where stress mani- fests itself. So you become tense and stiff and develop aching muscles, which, if left unattended, cause real physical problems in your organs and skeletal alignment. It is amazing what a single thought can lead to.

"It's all in the posture and tension of the body, and the more you become aware of how you hold yourself the greater the range of options you will have to develop a positive and confident mindset."

Posture and tension

- Think about your own body language and you will notice that you have some postures that you adopt whenever you are thinking in a particular way. It is amazing how precise these postures are, and the more habitual they become, the less aware of them you tend to be.

- NLP uses this knowledge for positive gain. If the mind works on the body in this way, then the body can be used to influence the mind. It is all in the posture and tension of the body, and the more you become aware of how you hold yourself the greater the range of options you will have to develop a positive and confident mindset.

- It really does not matter what type of body you have. So rather than putting all your effort into exercising your mind, you can share it with exercise for the body.

Stretching and breathing

In the West we often think that good exercise is about running and going to the gymnasium, but it really depends what you are doing as to whether you are gaining any benefit for your mind. If all your physical exercise is of the hard variety, such as weights and running on a treadmill, this may result in keeping your mind in its stuck place. To free your mind you need to exercise in a way that frees your body – using stretching and breathing exercises, as well as rotating movements such as you would learn from yoga or t'ai chi.

So look at your body from head to toe and identify some specific changes you could make to become more flexible and open in your thinking.

Follow the exercises in this chapter to free up your body – and your mind will follow.

Note: before you attempt the following take a quick check at how you are feeling now, and then compare this with how you feel after completing the adjustments suggested.

Head

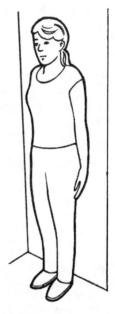

1 Pay attention to how you are holding your head when you are feeling low in confidence.

2 The more you allow your head to drop the worse you will feel.

3 Make a habit of keeping your head up with eyes focused on the horizon level or higher.

4 Just drop your chin a little.

5 You can get to this position easily by standing with your back against a wall.

6 Touch the wall with the back of your head, shoulder blades and heels.

7 Hold this posture and slowly walk away from the wall.

8 Relax, and make a point of relaxing your forehead and jaw, typically places where stress likes to collect. Be aware of how this feels as you relax.

This position is not only good for your posture, but will also reduce your negative inner voice and help you to stay on the field of play.

Shoulders

1 Check that your shoulders are at equal height when you look in the mirror.

2 If they are not, relax them and make an adjustment to even them up.

3 Notice how this feels and continue to make frequent adjustments each day.

4 Imagine releasing tension from the shoulders and feeling them sink down.

5 Raise them up and let them fall a few times so you get to feel the difference between elevated and relaxed shoulders.

Chest

1 Allow your chest to relax.

2 Let your arms hang down at your sides with the back of your hands relaxed and facing the front.

3 Slowly rotate your arms outward, and pull the shoulders back slightly so that the back of your hands end up facing sideways. You will notice your chest open and extend slightly. How do you feel as you make this small change?

Waist and hips

1 Stand with legs slightly apart as in the 'at ease' position.

2 Turn your waist from side to side a few times and again release any tension held there.

3 Increase the turning distance slightly with each turn and let your arms hang loose at your side.

4 Look in the mirror at the balance of your hips. Are they both at an equal height, or is one higher than the other?

5 Make any adjustment necessary to even them up.

Legs

1 Sit down as you would normally.

2 Observe your legs. Do you like to:

- tuck them underneath you

- have them stretched out in front

- crossed one over the other? If you cross them do you always have the same leg on top?

What is so important about body posture?

If you are feeling low in confidence there is every chance that your body is going to adopt the posture you always associate with this feeling. So by changing your posture you can change the way you feel.

Changing the way you feel by the way you sit

1 The next time you find yourself feeling low, pay attention to your legs.

2 Whatever configuration your legs are in, change them to be the opposite.

   (a) If they are crossed then cross them the opposite way.

   (b) If they are tucked under you stretch them out.

   (c) If they are stretched out place your feet flat on the floor in front of you.

3 You will be surprised at what a simple change like this can bring to your state of mind.

Breathing

For centuries meditation teachers have known that by changing your breathing you are able to directly change the way you are feeling.

■ When you were born, like all babies you began life by breathing deeply into your lower abdomen.

■ As life's experiences take their toll and we race to keep up with everything there is a tendency to breathe more shallowly.

■ When you are anxious or in a situation that makes you nervous your breathing is also likely to become more shallow, using only the upper part of your lungs.

Exercise: To encourage deep belly breathing

The next time you are feeling anxious, worried or stressed, pay attention to your breathing.

1 Stand in a quiet environment and take a deep breath. Notice how far down inside you take your breath.

2 Expand the lungs so that they compress the diaphragm below them and your belly (abdomen) expands.

3 Exhale gently through your nose.

4 As you breathe again through the belly feel your body relax and release tension from mind and body. This natural breathing pattern is good for oxygenating your blood and improving your circulation.

5 Practise more deep-belly breaths and, at the same time, relax your body at all the points indicated above. You should also feel a sunken rooted feeling. Notice how this makes you feel calmer and more grounded.

Use this very simple technique for remaining calm at times when you have tended to tense up and feel low in confidence.

Body gestures

Have you noticed how some people use their entire body in gestures as they speak? Watch an Italian or Spaniard in a lively conversation and you will see gesticulation in action. It is as if they would not be able to speak if you tied them to a chair. Confident speakers tend to use gestures to emphasise the points they want to get across, and it has been estimated that over half of our communication is interpreted from our body language and gestures.

Conversely, you will also have noticed other people who prefer to keep their body very still, as if scared of spilling out an emotion should they move too much. It is also true that people who do not use gestures, and keep their body language still, tend to be misunderstood more than most. They may feel that they have problems getting their message across because of the confused looks they get from those listening to them.

Vocal gestures

Over the telephone your chance of being misunderstood is increased even more. It is estimated that over a third of our communication is interpreted from the characteristics of our voice.

Think of your voice tone as being vocal gestures – and you can really begin to understand how to emphasise your point using changes in speed, volume and the tone of your voice (think back to the tone of voice on page 64). Conversely, the flatter your voice, the higher the chance of being misinterpreted. How flexible is your vocal range?

The looped pattern of confidence

Vocal tone is critical to confidence and in our programmes we have detected a common pattern of low confidence revolving around voice characteristics. This is how the pattern goes

I do not feel confident when speaking to other people.

My lack of confidence tends to affect my voice, which tails off in tone, speed and volume as I approach the end of what I am saying.

This causes the person I am speaking with to miss the end of my sentences and not fully understand what I am saying.

I notice the person's facial expression which I interpret as 'disinterested'.

I tail off even more and tell myself that I am not a confident speaker.

Hey presto – I have a self-fulfilling prophecy keeping me stuck in my feelings of low confidence and insecurity.

At least two people who had this pattern had decided on the belief that they had a mild form of Asperger syndrome (with its impaired emotional connections, lack of ability to interpret, and limited repetitive patterns of behaviour). We did not adopt this belief preferring to:

1 work with what was happening

2 create more awareness

3 offer techniques and procedures to improve vocal ability.

People will very often adopt the belief that they have a condition which then becomes a barrier to self-improvement. A label can become an excuse for a habit of poor articulation, and behind which you can resist doing anything to break out of the pattern. By giving a person a different way to communicate and working with what was happening rather than the belief (or diagnosis) they had adopted, we noticed marked improvements, especially where confidence was a key issue.

When illness becomes an excuse

Some people will make themselves ill in order to avoid something. It usually begins with a slight notion of a pain or feeling somewhere. The pain or discomfort is stirred up by your unconscious mind realising it needs an excuse for not doing something you have consciously said you would, or might do. Once this connection is made your symptoms grow stronger until you are incapacitated enough to justify non action. We also know this phenomenon by the well coined phrase 'psychosomatic illness'.

Body image: no quick fixes

Like most people you are probably bombarded with messages about health and fitness. New Year is a prime time when the media is full of messages about 'New Year, New You'. This is the time when you can make a fresh start, join a gym, begin a new diet and cleanse your mind. Another example is just before the summer holidays. It is time to lose a few pounds so you will look good on the beach, to get a pre-holiday tan and tone up your body.

The people behind these media campaigns know all too well how undisciplined many people are, constantly seeking labour-saving devices, and ways to make life easier. We seek faster foods, cars, entertainment, computers and, of course, faster fitness regimes. We want it now, and if one person will not give it to us we will get it somewhere else.

Compare the following two adverts. Which one is more appealing to you?

Quick, new way to optimum fitness.

No special diet or exercise required.

Lose weight as you sleep!

You will be amazed at the results after just two weeks following our easy plan to optimum fitness and health.

Special offer and money-back guarantee if not satisfied.

Work your way to optimum fitness.

If you stick to the special diet, do the quite strenuous exercises regularly you will eventually see some results.

If you do not have the discipline to keep to our regime forever you will not gain the full benefit.

Results are subject to your will power and determination.

"When you are able to have control over the parts of your mind and body that matter to you, you become less reliant on others and this in itself is confidence building."

The people who market health and fitness know the appeal of 'less effort is more attractive'. It is certainly true that some methods act faster than others, but newly gained fitness and health can easily slip back to the normal sluggishness as you fight to fit all the things you want to do into each day. The more you do the more something has to give. It is as if you have given up trying to be slim, smart or confident and you want someone else to do it for you.

The recent growth of hypnotherapy is due partly to people putting their faith in a process they do not have to be involved with – just do it to me! Whilst hypnotherapy is certainly very powerful in many areas, for long-term continuity there is no replacement for good old-fashioned will power, commitment and responsibility.

When you have control over the parts of your mind and body that matter to you, you become less reliant on others and this in itself is confidence building. To have the confidence that, no matter what the temptation, you are in control.

"When you learn to improve one thing, it can make you feel good. But when you learn to control your will power you can resist all kinds of things, and improve so many areas of your life."

Will power – the quantum leap to confidence

- Think back to a time when you did exercise control over your will and resisted a powerful temptation.

- Perhaps you resisted making a frivolous large purchase, or maybe the desire for a piece of chocolate, a cigarette or glass of wine.

- How did you feel after the event? Probably pretty good about yourself.

- When you learn to improve one thing, it can make you feel good. But when you learn to control your will power you can resist all kinds of things, and improve so many areas of your life.

- This is more of a quantum leap in building your confidence, rather than having to take it one step at a time.

... and stick to your promises

Every decision you make that you fail to follow through to action, and every promise you make that you later break will chip away at any confidence you have. You only have to let yourself down so many times that eventually you stop making decisions and promises so that you stop failing. Smokers frequently procrastinate over stopping because they want to avoid adding one more failure to their experience. The way to build confidence back up is to stick like superglue to the things that you decide and promise.

Exercise: To develop strong will power

■ Read through this exercise and commit it to memory, then do the exercise in one take.

■ If you break off part way through it may not have the full effect.

■ Ideally do it with someone else, to facilitate this exercise for you, so you can concentrate fully on doing the exercise and not keep having to refer to the instructions.

1 Recall a time when you were able to resist a powerful temptation, and where you felt really good about the decision you made. Take your time and think of something that brings up positive feelings as you think about it now.

2 Focus on this event and notice the qualities of the visual memory you have as you remember how good you were feeling.

3 Now answer the following questions on the 'quality' of the vision and sound. Pay special attention to these qualities as you will come back to this image shortly.

(a) Whereabouts in your mind's eye does the memory appear?

(b) How big is the image you are looking at? Notice how colourful and bright it is.

(c) Are you hearing any sounds? If so what tone, high or low? From where is the sound coming? How loud is it?

4 Now think of some part of your life where you would like to have more self-control. Choose something meaningful to you that you have been wanting for some time.

5 When you have decided on something notice the qualities of the memory – location, size, colour, brightness and sound (tone, location and volume).

6 Take this second memory and slowly move it into the exact location of the first memory which has the good feelings

associated with it. As you do so have this second memory take on all the visual and auditory qualities of the first – so the picture and sound remains the same, but the location, size, colour, brightness and sound are changed to that of the first image.

7 Take your time and make sure that you get all these qualities exactly the same.

8 Now, how do you feel about taking control over this aspect of your life? Where is this feeling?

9 Why not strengthen the feeling by imagining it growing inside you and shooting around your body going up through your neck and down to the very tips of your fingers and toes.

10 Send it around and around faster and faster. How does this feel now you are taking control over this aspect of your life?

How long do you want to stay confident for?

When you think about being confident do you see yourself as you are now, or are you older? This is an important question, because your mind is very good at getting you what you want, but once you have it, there may be no real impetus to keep hold of it. When you programme your mind to improve things for you, it is wise to tell it how long you want the improvement for.

Exercise: for healthy eating over a given period

Imagine you want to eat more healthily. You might create a picture in your mind of making a healthy meal for dinner tomorrow. You might even have taken this picture from a cookery book – probably written by a celebrity chef! This picture is enough to get you into the local store to buy the fresh food you need which you bring home, cook and enjoy! Job well done, loop closed.

The next day you have to work late and pick up a pizza on the way home. The next day you feel a little tired and before you know it you are back eating chips in front of the television.

So the next time you create a picture of a healthy meal go one step further.

1 Imagine how healthy you will be when you are eating like this regularly.

2 See yourself five years down the line looking very healthy.

3 Then go another five years, then ten more.

4 See yourself at the ripe age of 65 still healthy and fit as a fiddle.

5 Then go to 75, then 85, then 90 still healthy, still walking about fit as a fiddle. We know you have learned not to let any limiting beliefs about age get in the way.

There are plenty of people on the planet walking about fit as a fiddle at the age of 90, and our life expectancy is extending year by year. So why would you not still be healthy at 95? How about 100?

Remember, 'Age is a state of mind.'

The more you imagine yourself healthy, fit, agile and confident at a ripe age, the more your mind will get you to do the things you need to do to get there. Sadly, it is more common for the reverse to be the norm. Many people expect to get old, stiffen up and become frail. So guess what? This is exactly what happens to them. You need not be included in this statistic.

NLP TRIGGER

YOUR MIND AND BODY ARE PART OF THE SAME SYSTEM

- The mind is clearly part of your body.

- When you have a thought you raise an emotion which is a bodily sensation, a visceral activity in your body somewhere.

- The two are connected in such a way that it is impossible for even one thought not to affect your body in some way.

- When you move your body try not to have a thought. If you just tense your little toe just a fraction you have to engage your mind to do so. Even the movements you make, which you are unaware of, are controlled by the unconscious part of your mind.

- Mind and body are more often thought of as one entity rather than two, so the part of you that remembers how to ride a bike or type a letter is as much in your muscles and tendons as it is in the part of you that you call your brain.

- The way to a long and happy life is to imagine having it first – then keep those images alive!

Imagine successful outcomes

"Obstacles are those frightful things you see when you
take your eyes off your goal."
Henry Ford, founder of the Ford motor company

What you have discovered so far

- You can use your body to reveal the amazing capacity of your mind.
- Every single thought you have transfers its attitude into your body.
- Flexible, open minds speak with flexible and open body language.
- Posture, gestures and breathing can be used to develop self-confidence.
- The promise of an effortless solution is very appealing, but nowhere near as effective as the discipline of 'doing-it-yourself'.
- The stronger the will power, the greater the self-confidence.

What you are going to discover

- Being absolutely clear about what it is you want to use your confidence for, day by day and week by week, is going to be crucial to your success. You need a goal to aim for.
- The way to think about any goal is not so much about what you want to achieve, but about what outcomes you would like as a result of achieving it.
- You can give your outcomes an increased chance of success by describing them in such a way that they are well formed in your mind – 'framing' them with positive visualisations.

Directing the movie in your mind's eye

The trouble with focusing on goals is that they lie in the future and getting there requires foresight. It can be a little like looking up at the mountain and imagining how much hard work it will be to climb it. But how about reframing the time frame instead?

– What if you could see a film taken from the top of the mountain showing all the possible routes you could take?

– Even better, what if you could experience being on top of the mountain, as if you had already made the climb and arrived at the peak?

Well there is actually nothing to stop you from doing this. In fact this is exactly what top athletes, including mountain climbers, do before setting off on a race or a climb. They picture doing it in their mind, and they feel a sense of achievement, of having succeeded, and this increases their motivation and energy to succeed.

Exercise: Creating a time frame for your desired outcome

Rather than looking towards your future goal, whatever it may be, how would it feel to imagine you have already achieved it? You can use physical distance to represent the time between now and your future goal, making achieving your goal feel more real.

1 Write your goal on an orange circle.

2 Place an object on the floor to represent 'now'.

3 Pace out the distance that you feel represents the length of time it will take you to achieve your goal.

4 Place your orange circle on the ground at this point.

5 As you turn around and look back at 'now' you will be able to imagine with greater clarity what you did to succeed.

Case study: Make sure your outcome is what you want, not what other people want for you

When Tanni Grey-Thompson first realised she was not going to be able to walk by herself at the age of seven, her physicians set a goal for her – to walk again. They decided that Tanni would be given every possible aid to enable her to walk upright. She was fitted with what Tanni later described as extremely uncomfortable callipers which restricted her movement in every way. Much time, energy and money was spent in refining the callipers to help her to walk upright. Had they stopped to ask Tanni about her outcome they could have saved themselves a lot of trouble. Tanni had a strong independent streak as a young girl and had her own outcomes in her mind – she wanted to be mobile so that she could get on with lots of things. **Being upright was not important; being able to move around at high speed was**. The day she received her first wheelchair, she says, was one of the happiest days of her life – she could now get around at much higher speeds, and she went on to become an Olympic champion. Today she is Dame Tanni Grey-Thompson DBE, one of the most successful athletes in the UK (check out http://www.tanni.co.uk/).

Sometimes the things you want to do may seem insurmountable, not because of the size or difficulty of any particular challenge, but because of the way you are approaching it. It is very common for parents to want a vulnerable child to be more mature and sure of themselves, but often their efforts to shape and mould the child into an image they have in their heads can have the opposite effect.

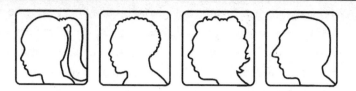

Case study: Learning to be yourself

Stephan was a personal development trainer and specialised in speaking to large groups of business people. Only in his early thirties Stephan was becoming exhausted and could not understand how his peers could deliver similar programmes to his without the loss of energy he was experiencing. During our NLP sessions with Stephan, he referred to the people he was training as 'his audience'. This suggested that he could be seeing himself as an actor, or motivational speaker, having to maintain a high energy role. Consequently, he put himself under a good deal of pressure to 'perform' on stage. He measured his success on the quality of his personal performance. We suggested that, if he was in the personal development business, would it not be better to consider his 'audience' as learners thus transferring the focus from him to them. If he were to consider their learning needs and focus on ways of achieving them he could take away the pressure he was imposing on himself to act.

There are many ways to begin new ventures. Which will be the most appropriate method for you?

"The mind has a habit of gravitating towards the things you programme into it."

How to think through your outcomes

Both Tanni and Stephan were victims of outcomes that had not been properly thought through (by others or themselves).

Whether you are going to a meeting, having a party, making a telephone call, planning a holiday, preparing for a presentation, psyching up for a difficult conversation, changing your career, delivering news or deciding to help a colleague or friend, it is always advisable to make sure that you have an outcome in mind and that the outcome is well formed. Being able to visualise your completed outcome in detail helps you to stay focused and on track.

Here are some key steps you need to include to help you frame a well-formed outcome.

1 **Focus on a positive outcome.**

- State what you want in positive terms.

- For a meeting you want to go well, for example, this would go something like, 'I want the meeting to run smoothly so I will make sure that everyone is clear about the outcome we are aiming to achieve, and I will use my meeting skills to keep people on track.'

- The mind has a habit of gravitating towards the things you programme into it – so block out any negative thoughts. For example, if you say to yourself, 'I do not want to make a mess of this meeting,' what your mind will register is 'mess of this meeting' and, guess what happens? Yes, you will probably make a mess of the meeting. Rephrase in the positive with, 'I want this meeting to achieve its purpose.'

2 **Tap in to your internal and external resources.** For a successful meeting outcome (to continue the example), do you have both the external and internal resources to achieve your outcome?

- External resources would include such things as an appropriate venue, agenda, meeting notes, pens, paper, water and so on.

- Internal resources may include confidence, patience and the ability to speak clearly, listen effectively, take everyone's views into account and summarise decision points.

3 **Practise the NLP techniques already grasped.** By now you will know that you can give yourself these resources by using the NLP techniques covered in the previous chapters.

For example, you could:

- use some orange circle thinking to collapse a previous negative experience of running a meeting; or you may want to

- set yourself an anchor for patience if you know you have someone who likes to go into a lot of detail at the meeting. You could of course anticipate this, and ensure that comprehensive notes are prepared and circulated at the end of the meeting to reassure those who love to revel in detail.

4 **Factor in your skills level.** You also want to check you have appropriate skills. Do not over-egg them either: if you have ever watched TV programmes such as *The X Factor* or *Pop Idol* you will have seen contestants pumped up with pseudo-confidence only to make a fool of themselves in front of the judges and millions of viewers as they open their mouth and begin to sing. Confidence is important, but so are skills. Skills can be learned through training and development. In the example of a meeting, have you managed one before? Have you watched how others do it successfully? Have you checked your resources? Make sure you are investing in the skills you need to succeed in your chosen area.

5 **Maintain control of your outcome.** Retain control of your outcome even if you enlist the help of other people. If you are dependent on outside sources to succeed, then keep track of what they are doing for you, so that if things begin to go off course you can intervene to offer support and maybe make a necessary correction. Never assume you are the top priority for other people. It is surprising how quickly a person's priorities and loyalties can change.

6 **Consider the consequences.** It is always good to check the impact that achieving your outcome will have on the following:

■ other people

■ the environment.

If you achieve your outcome will it have a negative impact on your family, friends, team, organisation or the physical environment? Of course, not everything you do will be ecologically sound for everyone – if it was you would never leave the house for fear of polluting the atmosphere in some way, no one would ever be removed from their role, and dysfunctional relationships would continue for ever!

The secret here is to do your utmost to ensure that your outcome is ecologically sound, that on balance the benefits are positive and, if someone or something is not going to benefit from it, then ask yourself whether you can live with the consequences. If the answer is 'yes' then go ahead.

"What the mind conceives the body can achieve."

7 **Create the all-singing, all-dancing, technicolour picture.** Spend some quality time in this phase of your outcome.

■ Create a picture in your mind of what you will see, hear and feel when you have completed your outcome.

■ Put in every last detail, make it big and colourful, imagine what you will hear and associate fully with the picture so that you can feel a real sense of success.

■ For the example of a successful meeting, you may see people leaving the meeting, energised and buzzing, congratulating you on your effective running of the meeting.

■ You could create a mind movie of the whole event – people discussing, listening and maintaining a high level of energy throughout the meeting, pausing for comfort breaks and coffee.

■ The difference between holding an image of success and an image of failure in your mind is personal choice. There really is nothing preventing you from imagining a successful outcome first, before leaping into action.

■ People who are used to failing usually know they are going to do so. They have imagined failing. They have told themselves how difficult it is going to be, and how other people will not be interested.

8 **Time out.** Make sure you put a timescale on what it is you are trying to achieve. A phenomenon of well-formed outcomes is that they often come to fruition ahead of time as the mind begins to work unconsciously towards them.

Exercise: To embed and gain more clarity around your well-formed outcome

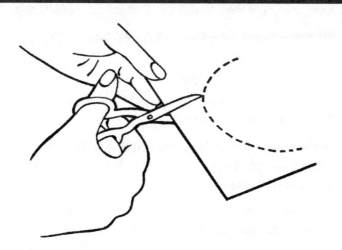

1 Write your outcome on an orange circle cut from a piece of card.

2 Place a marker on the floor to represent 'now'.

3 Walk forward in a straight line to a spot that represents the time when you will have achieved your outcome.

4 Place the orange circle on the spot and stand behind it looking back to 'now'.

5 Imagine you have already achieved your outcome and you are looking back into the past (that is, 'now').

6 Enjoy the moment of having achieved your outcome. Imagine the 'sensory-based evidence' you identified whilst setting your outcome. Associate fully with it ... feel it deeply, and enjoy it for a few minutes.

Self-test for judging how well you achieved your outcome

Take your time with each of these questions. Your answers will increase your motivation and make it easier for you to achieve your outcome.

1 What impact has this successful outcome had on how you feel about yourself?

2 Have your values changed in any way? Has achieving your outcome given you a greater sense of what is important? Has it consolidated your values?

3 What beliefs did you change in order to achieve your outcome? What new empowering beliefs do you have now that you have achieved your outcome?

4 Knowing that you are capable of this achievement how much more are you capable of?

5 What are you doing differently now that you have achieved your outcome? Are you behaving differently, have you taken on new responsibilities?

6 How has your environment changed as a result of your achievement? How have people been affected? How are they relating to you? Are things different from before?

Conclusion: remember

- The more you get into the habit of setting well-formed outcomes, the more your mind and body will know what you want it to do.

- You will find your confidence building day by day as your mind gravitates towards completing the outcomes you set for it.

- You will find yourself setting outcomes that increasingly will stretch and challenge you in different ways.

NLP TRIGGER

THERE IS NO OBJECTIVE REALITY – ONLY YOUR UNIQUE INDIVIDUAL PERCEPTION OF WHAT YOU BELIEVE IS REAL AND TRUE

- Saying that what is 'out there' is not really out there, but is just in your mind, may seem like bad news.

- But think of it this way: every single person on this earth is creating their own perception in their mind of what they believe reality is. So, pessimists believe reality has a way of making things turn out for the worst, and optimists believe reality has a way of making things turn out for the best.

■ Who is right? Right and wrong do not come into it, because there is no objective reality – only your perception of it. So this should be good news because it means you have a choice about how you decide to perceive the world, and what you believe about it.

■ Use well-formed outcomes and the power of your imagination to put some good stuff Into your life.

11

The confidence challenge

"A person can grow only as much as his horizon allows."
John Powell, film composer

What you have discovered so far

■ That true confidence is being comfortable
  with yourself to engage with areas
  outside your safety zone and 'have a go'.

■ You can take the confidence you have in one context and transfer it to
  situations where it is lacking.

■ There are simple strategies and exercises to help rebuild confidence
  that is knocked out of you.

■ Self-awareness leads to self-belief.

■ You need to stay 'on the field of engagement' and connect with others.

■ Body confident is mind confident.

■ You can create empowering feelings and stamp out negativity.

■ How to handle illusion and make your own reality.

What you are going to discover

■ How you experience each day will depend upon how you wake up,
  and your commitment to using all the techniques and exercises
  provided for you in this book.

■ You can put all this into practice now with a simple short challenge.

Can you handle the confidence challenge?

1 We are calling it a challenge because this is the way we want
  you to approach it. Something else to explore, and another
  'confidence win' to add to all the wins you are already
  experiencing.

2 We are encouraging you to create your own challenges, to
  stretch and widen your horizons and take bigger leaps outside
  your comfort zone.

3 If you have read this book and are a little overwhelmed trying to think of which exercise to use for which situation, this challenge will help you to be clearer about taking the next steps, building your confidence day by day, hour by hour, and minute by minute.

4 To help you do this we have suggested a 'workout' to follow from the moment you wake up each day, to the moment your head hits the pillow at night.

5 If you commit to following this workout every day for two weeks we guarantee that you will feel increasingly confident (and this will translate into more achievements and successes in your life).

Confidence challenge – a daily routine

1 **Preparation.** First of all prepare your environment by placing a confidence anchor somewhere in your bedroom where you will see it the moment you wake up. You might like the idea of an orange circle to remind you to step into your confidence routine, or something with which you associate confident feelings. The idea is for you to see this object as soon as you awake and for it to remind you that today you are going to feel more confident.

2 **'Rise and shine'.** Before you get out of your bed look at your confidence anchor and tell yourself, in positively stated internal dialogue, that today you are going to feel confident, regardless of what the world has in store for you. Now think ahead to your day and choose one scenario where you are going to be more confident than you have been in the past. Focus on this event.

3 **Get ready to take on the day.** Now, as you carry out your morning bathroom and breakfast routine, prepare yourself for this event by running through the following checklist. Mentally rehearse the event using **Exercise: To embed and gain more**

clarity around your well-formed outcome (at the end of Chapter 10) with an orange circle (this should take you about 10 minutes).

(a) Check your posture. Keep your head up, stay relaxed and be focused.

(b) Check your internal dialogue. Make sure it is positive.

(c) Be aware of any comparison you might make and stop it.

(d) No judging of anything. Just be curious to learn.

4 **Seize the day**. You are meeting the day head on. Whatever it has in store for you is okay because you have your 'bring it on' state with which to connect with all the events that are about to unfold.

(a) Remember to stay relaxed, breathe deeply and take things a little more slowly than usual.

(b) Check your state. Confidence requires positive states of mind. Make sure you are in an appropriate positive state before doing anything. Remember – state, state and more state management.

(c) Have your confidence anchor ready to use should you need it.

(d) Frame every new event in the positive, for example, 'I'm going to the meeting with a positive attitude to learn more about (X) and put over my views confidently.'

(e) Be prepared to reframe your thinking if you find negativity creeping in.

(f) Be open to listening to yourself, in particular if any negative illusions you may be constructing about people, events or yourself are voicing themselves. Have a zero-tolerance policy on your negative illusions, including any judgements you might make. Instead of judging – stay curious.

5 **How was it for you?** At the end of your day, review how things went.

- ▨ Give yourself a mental 'thumbs up' for what you did to bolster your confidence, and remember where you want to make improvements.

- ▨ Make sure that your review is positive and be kind to yourself; do not dwell on what did not go so well, instead tell yourself how you will do differently next time and be determined to make progress each day.

- ▨ Spend your review time 'bigging yourself up' (using your internal dialogue, not out loud to other people). If you have a partner or friend who is supporting you in your quest for confidence then by all means talk to them about your day – and keep it positive.

- ▨ Finally, anchor any positive feelings of confidence so you can feel this way more of the time.

After this review, just prime yourself with this thought from the children's author Dr Seuss:

You have brains in your head

You have feet in your shoes

You can steer yourself in any direction you choose

LUCAN LIBRARY TEL. 6216422